CW01496697

Mon~~strous Creatur~~es:

Monsters

&

Creatures.

True Tales

Steph Young

Table of Contents

Introduction

In the Supernatural & Cryptozoological worlds of the strange, it's unusual to find new entities. Ghosts, demons, and creatures of the night, that come to life straight from our very nightmares, or beasts we once thought purely mythical, will often reappear and rear their heads once more; but recently, there seems to have been an emergence of new, or perhaps never reported entities. Monstrous creatures... and we know not what they are....

Who is Steph Young?

Steph Young is a frequent guest on radio shows & podcasts including appearances on the National Radio show 'Coast to Coast AM,' as well as many more...

Steph is an independent researcher, addicted to researching all Supernatural, Paranormal, Esoteric and Enigmatic Unexplained Mysteries. Each book she writes seems to lead her to further questions and searches for answers, as the Unexplained Mysteries inevitably deepen & develop into ever more complex riddles in the spectrum of the Unknown.

Steph Young now hosts a Podcast on iTunes. "Masquerade podcast with steph young" discussing creepy mysteries of the Unexplained," covering all unexplained mysteries, unexplained disappearances, all things paranormal, encounters with the unknown, unsolved mysteries, and of course, creepy Monsters, and strange things that happen in the woods...

Free Episodes are now up on Itunes, or more episodes are on Patreon at 'Masquerade Podcast with steph young.'

Chapter One: The Stick Men

One of these Monstrous Creatures appears to be the 'Black Stick Men.' The spirit seekers blog believes they are many, and many have seen them…. black 'stick men,' like children draw, but very real, and very big. Incredibly tall and thin jet-black stick figures, with no faces. Their heads are just a black mass with no facial features. Their walk is often described as a "lolloping" gait. Their appearances have started to be described in just the last couple of years. They move silently, smoothly, eerily gliding. Are they real? Are they really new? If so, why would they show up now? Or, wonders the spirit seekers, have they always been here but are choosing to show themselves only now? If so, what do they want with us?

Kathy Casey says: "In May 2013, I was coming out of my studio behind my house when I saw movement. My studio is behind my house at about a distance of 60 feet. It was dark; the only lights on were coming from my porch but they weren't enough to cast a shadow. I saw a very tall, solid shadow, with no features. It was very thin, about thirteen feet tall, moving fast. I could see its outline. It had an elongated head and its arms and fingers were very long and thin. It was solid. It was taking large steps. It was fast – almost a run. I could see no facial features; but this was not a shadow; it was solid. It was upright, moving fast. It was out of my reference - I felt like it was old and alien. I'm not easily frightened ...but now I think twice before going outside at night..."

Sandy says: "In April 2012, living in Charleston with 4 acres of woods on both sides of my home, it was around 1 am and I was out on my porch with my dog.

Suddenly I saw movement in the yard and my dog made a little bark and then looked mesmerized as was I as we watched three tall black figures glide across the yard. It lasted a few seconds. They were tall stick figures and then they just vanished into the trees."

"My husband is 6'4 and they were at least a foot and a half taller. I sat there, then grabbed a flashlight and walked out into the yard. I was nervous not knowing what I saw. These black stick figures were darker than the night. There is no light in the yard or from the house. I could see them - they had long thin arms and fingers with odd shaped heads and they had no faces. They all were the same height and all looked exactly alike."

This happened at night, but, on another occasion, something even worse happened. "I was out on the porch in daylight, in the morning. Then, when I was on my computer and when I shut it off, you know how the screen goes black? Well, over my shoulder I saw one of the black figures, for maybe 2 seconds. I gasped and it was gone. It was the exact same black stick figure but only one of them this time."

As if to defend herself from skeptics, she adds, "I'm in my forties and college educated. I have a good head on my shoulders. I know what I saw. Whatever it is – they are watching."

After hearing me talk of these entities on a radio show, a man named Clint contacted me recently to relate his series of strange events: "I was born in Granite City, Illinois, across the river from St. Louis MO. I spent most of my life in the inner city till I was 12 years old when we moved into the south central of Missouri Ozark's. For me it felt surreal, being in the country after a 12-year-old life-time in a concrete jungle. As a child of the city, you were always afraid to walk alone at night. We carried weapons, travelled in groups for protection, had escape routes planned out where we could disappear fast in miles and miles of what seemed to me to be endless humanity.'

'Then, at 12 years old, that all changed. I felt safe walking old country roads at night. Houses could be 2 or 3 miles apart instead of cramped and packed in together. You could walk all night and never see anyone. At School my older brother and I made friends with some neighbours about three miles from us. My older brother was more friendly with Bruce, who was more his age, and I made friends with Paul, he being more my age.'

'One Saturday, I got bored and decided to walk to my friend's house, which I didn't do much cause it was a long walk, but off I went, and when I get there my older brother is already there talking to Bruce who is obviously still in a state of shock and fear by the look on his face.'

'He told us; "Something followed me last night while I was walking home. I thought it was a squirrel at first, then it came closer, got heavier, like a cow, then even closer and heavier. It kept pace with me through the woods till I came to a field and I thought I'd die when it would show itself but, there was nothing to see. It's still next to me only 10-20 feet away but, there's nothing to see and this thing must be as big as an Elephant by now." I remember thinking OMG I hope that never happens to me, and the look of fear on Bruce's face haunted me anytime I walked dark country roads after that.'

'In time however I forgot about it, walking county roads at night (when I had to) was peaceful, relaxing. I enjoyed the solitude. Then, one night, fifteen years later in 1985, when I'm 27 years old, it happened to me. I had an old beat-up pick-up truck that I only used for short trips because it had a tendency to fail me on occasion and I'd have to leave it on the side of the road till the next day when it would decide it would serve me once again and start back up and run just fine. About three miles from my house was an all-night truck stop called the Oasis which had gotten honourable mention in the Garth Brooks song "Friends in Low Places" and I had gone there to meet a friend that never showed, so, I left there about 3 a.m. About half a mile from there my old truck once again failed me. No big deal, I'm only three miles from home, so I leave it where it stalled and start walking.'

'It was one of those nights when the moonshine is so bright you can see your own shadow and can see for miles. About five minutes after I start walking it started. Quiet at first, it starts deep in a thick of woods and its keeping pace with me, which unnerves me. During the day it would have been hard to keep pace in the tangle of woods, but, at night would be impossible, it made me aware that this was unnatural, whatever this was whether squirrel or deer, should not be able to keep pace with me like this at night. It very quickly started coming closer through the woods and I became aware that this (thing) was bipedal, walking on two feet, as it came closer. I move to the other side of the road and keep my eyes on the woods as I walk.'

'Up ahead around a bend in the road is a field that someone had bulldozed a section of woods into a deep hollow at the far end of the field. As I come to this clearing I tell myself that whatever this is will be plain to see in the moonlight once it's out of the wood's and it'll be something I should have known or expected would be there and I'd feel silly that I, a grown man, had been afraid in the first place.'

'But, from the sounds it made in the woods, I knew that was not going to happen. Situations like this make a person cast about for a reason. You tell yourself that it's anything except what you can see or hear (or not see). However, when I did come to the clearing it got worse. It came closer, was louder, from the sound it made; It must be a couple ton's. I'd heard cattle run before, and they make a heavy sound from their weight, but this was much heavier, and like I've said, bipedal.'

'Now it's out in the open and I still can't see whatever this is. I'm on the far side of the road and this is from what I can hear no more than thirty feet away, just on the other side of the fence and I should be able to see something, but, there's just this LOUD thumping sound It makes as It walks next to me. If I walk faster, It walks faster, If I slow, It slows, If I stop, It stops. I then remember back all those years ago of the look of fear on my friend Bruce's face and how I'd felt dread that such a thing should ever happen to me, and now I'm thinking, this is real, this is happening.'

'By now the fear is so palpable. If I'd had a knife I could have cut you off a piece and handed it to you, but, in spite of instinct to run, I keep a façade of calm and just walk, running would give whatever this was reason to give chase. I keep walking by force of will and keep my eyes on the field next to me and my sights on the brush pile at the end of the half-mile long field, there are whole trees in that pile and it's twice as high as my house; whatever this was had to stop once I got there. But, it didn't. It just kept on going straight through the brush pile tearing up country as it did. Now, I could try and explain the sound of a five-ton spook tearing through brush but there's just no way to describe It. POW, POP, SNAP. Still not good enough. But, I will tell you this, once and once only. I screamed, like a school girl and took off running. I've never done that before you know, screamed in fear I mean.'

'It stands to reason that it must have stopped following me, I mean, I'm still here, but, I don't remember the run the rest of the way home. I don't think I was abducted or anything like that, my opinion is that I was fear blanked. This is no-where near the end of this story. I've talked to several people with similar stories of what I think is this same creature that I now call stick man.'

'A couple months after my encounter I was talking to my brother and told him what had happened and half expected him to call bull..., cause that's how he is, one of those people that doesn't believe in anything. Anyway, he told me that around the same time (different night) he and his friend Steve were sitting on the hood of their car down by the Gasgonade river which is just outside our town and near where I'd had my scare, when they started to notice that they were hearing a noise across the river on the other side of a field that was next to the one were I'd had my scare.'

'He said it started up top of a wooded hill about a half mile from where they sat. It was loud enough that they could hear it from that distance as it came down the hill and into an open field and continued toward them, getting louder all the way the whole time and, as with me, there's nothing to see, and, like me, they can't get their heads around that fact. "We can't see anything," he told me, and from the sound of it there should be a house walking toward them. It finally crossed the field and came to the line of brush that grew along the river and tore through the brush to the river and jumped in and started toward them and the whole time, there's nothing to see even though he and his friend could see the splash It made as It swam toward them.'

'While he was telling me this story he told me he had an overpowering urge to get in the car and beat it outta there long before It made it halfway across the field, but, being young and all that, he wasn't going to be the first to turn tail and run, not with his friend there. It was when It jumped in the water and started swimming toward them that they both lost their nerve, jumped into the car and fish tailed it outta there.'

'Now comes the story of Jack. Jack was a tattooed hippie type that once told me during a conversation about whatever this was that had followed me and scared my brother that he (Jack) welcomed the unknown no matter how dark. Yeah, he was a little on the scary side. We were having these conversations every morning because I was Jack's ride to work and every morning he would walk to my house have coffee and kill time till it was time to leave for work. He lived about a mile from me outside of town and sometime during the first week he started riding with me to work he just sort of mentioned in an off-hand don't care kinda way tells me: "Something followed me in the woods this morning; it does every morning."

'When I ask about it he tells me basically the same story that my brother and I shared. He told me it started the first day he started walking to my house to catch a ride to work. "If I'm walking next to the field, It's in the woods. If I walk next to the wood's, It's in the field," he told me. He said It was there every morning. When I ask if he could see it, he said he thought It was hiding from him because he was trying to get a look at It. He told me; "When It's on the other side of the road in the wood's I try and surprise It and jump to the other side of the road and It appears to go into the field. Then I jump to the other side where the field is and It goes back into the woods."

'It went like that for a couple months, then one morning he comes in for coffee and tells me; "I saw It. It was in the woods and when I jumped to the side of the road where It was this morning, It didn't go to the other side into the field this time. It was behind a tree and It moved so fast that it was a blur but It would stop long enough for me to get a good look at It."

'Jack told me It was 8-9 feet tall and was black and looked like a stick man, the kind of stick figure we used to draw as children in school. He said It moved so fast that It wavered into a blur as It moved back and forth between trees and that's what made the sound of loud walking that my brother and I had heard, then It would stop so he could see It, standing still for a few seconds, then start the blurry wavy movement again. Since then my friends and I just call It stick man.'

'This all happened a long time ago. I don't walk county roads much these days but every once in awhile I hear someone brag that they're not scared of anything and that they're gonna go out in the woods and dare any kinda bogie to show itself. My advice is, don't go, you'll find what you're looking for......'

Rob Bobson describes what happened to him; "When I was 13, my parents sent me to a farming school in South Africa. I loved the freedom - every weekend by myself, I would hunt and fish and have fun. This was my life for the first few months there. It was bliss. Then one day, a day I will never forget, I went down to the river with friends to swim."

"It was a Saturday, a normal day, but we noticed that the clouds were rolling in and so we began the very long walk back. When we were about half way back, and feeling tired, we all said that we suddenly felt as if we were being watched, but we looked around and there was nothing was there, and we carried on walking back for a few minutes."

"It was starting to rain and we got that feeling again, and we stood there for about a minute looking hard around the forest, behind us, and just as we were about to carry on walking, a tall, featureless black creature crossed the path about twenty meters behind us. It was like nothing I had ever seen before; the way it walked, it was like it was gliding, and it was moving extremely fast. None of us moved or spoke; then the fear set in and we ran all the way back. The next day we all spoke about what we'd seen, and we all agreed we had all seen the same thing..."

Cody thinks he saw one. "Me and a friend were traveling on a dirt road in the mountains in Idaho. We were stopping at a gas station, and as we pulled in, my friend said, "What the ...?' then... Oh, never mind."

"When I pulled the car up to the gas pump and got one foot out the car to go to the pump, something made a very loud frightening noise, like a sort of clicking noise and I saw the trees shake. I jumped back in the car and we took off! Down the road, I saw it move quickly toward the car from the edge of the road. I just kept moving, kept driving. I didn't say anything. I kept silent until an hour or so later when I told my friend what I thought I'd just seen. He said he'd seen the same thing standing near the pump when we pulled up but it had run off. He said he thought it was his eyes playing tricks on him. The weird thing was - it killed the car stereo, and my cell phone battery. It made the lights at the gas pump glow very bright. What I saw looked like a stick figure drawn on a white-board."

A lady from Tennessee recently called the Mutual UFO Network, not knowing who else to call and needing to urgently talk about what had just happened to her that morning. It was around 6am and she was standing on the deck of her house drinking an early morning coffee, enjoying the warm and quiet beginning to her day, when suddenly she saw something that defied explanation.

The deck of her house was at an elevation of twelve feet from the ground below. When she turned around to go back into the house, she stopped dead. She could not fail to see the huge black shadow; the shape of a man but standing higher than the deck. It was leaning against it. It was the shape of a man yet it appeared to have no face. She was frozen to the spot, unable to move.

Suddenly it turned its 'head' toward her. Then she watched as very slowly it peeled itself off the rail. It ran its fingers slowly along the side of the rail as though it was coming in her direction. Then it started floating away.

It had legs but it wasn't touching the ground as it walked. It moved its legs like a man would. Then as it got some distance away, it turned back around in her direction again. She felt very sure that it was communicating the message to her that though it had left her unharmed; it was more than capable of hurting her if it chose to do so...

Mary Margaret Zimmer of the Mutual UFO Network in Florida writes about a CCTV camera capturing a peculiar set of images. In July 2005, she received footage sent to her from Kelantan, Malaysia. It had been captured from a private CCTV camera installed on top a tall apartment building.

The film footage showed a mysterious hazy black mass of no definite clear shape, just a dark mass, estimated to be approximately 3-4 feet by 2-3 feet. It was moving, crawling fast over roof tops. It scaled walls and moved with speed, faster than any animal. It was using its hands and legs and scaled up a long drainage pipe. Upon reaching the top, it then scaled back down nimbly and fast, again faster than a human would be able to. When it crossed the roofs it appeared to be on all fours, but it was faster than any primate. Oddly, while the building walls and roof tops were clearly in focus, whatever the entity was itself, it appeared blurry on the footage and no features could be clearly seen, as though it were masking its true form.

On Pararesearchers.org of Ontario, Andy contributes his extraordinary encounter which happened in London. 'Early on a weekday morning when I was a student, my friend and I were walking back to my house from another friend's house where we'd spent the night revising. No alcohol or drugs or alcohol had been involved. We were very tired and didn't talk as we entered my street. Dawn was breaking and I saw a man coming towards us in the distance.

"See that man? He isn't a man, is he?" I asked my friend.

She replied, "No."

Did I just say that?"

"You did. He isn't."

'The figure had changed. It was all black, like a silhouette and now it was very very thin and had very long arms. It was taking lolloping dancing steps. It didn't have a face. We freaked. We ran. I rushed through the front door and we ran inside. The front door was glass. It pressed up against the glass. We couldn't breathe.'

'It stayed for what felt like an eternity, before suddenly disappearing. One second it wasn't gone. It was definitely not of the world we know. This was not imagined; it was real and we both felt great fear. We also felt it was like it had changed form as though its 'glamour' had gone; its innate ability to become invisible, and it was angry. I never want to see it again, whatever dimensions it came from...'

What are these strange figures, and why do they sometimes generate the impression that they are ancient beings?

Spanish Paranormal Radio Show Mira Lo Oculto (See the Unseen) reported on an odd incident experienced by a couple in January 2005, near Getafe; half an hour's drive south of Madrid in Spain. The man and his girlfriend were in their car and were parked along a quiet and isolated road.

Suddenly the man observed a strange shadowy shape moving near the car. His girlfriend then saw the shadowed figure. They said that it seemed to be moving and that it was in one spot one moment and then instantaneously it would appear in a different spot. At one point, it came right up to the car and seemed to be peering in, though no face was visible.

After it moved away again, the shocked and frightened man found the courage to get out of the car and walk around, perplexed by who or what it could be, but on hearing shuffling noises in the grass by the car he lost his nerve and ran back into the car. The noise was coming from different directions at the same time.

He started the car engine and put it into reverse, keen to get away from the eerie place. The shadowy thing was still in sight, moving at great speed from one place to another, and they could see it was the average height of a man, yet it moved so fast. Despite the headlights lighting the area in front of the car, the figure did not look any clearer and they could still not see its true form. The man drove backwards and on reaching the end of the road, began to drive away fast, both of them too scared to remain any longer.

When they arrived home, they parked up and as they were leaving the car, the man noticed that across the windshield, among the mist from the cold night air, were two hand prints, clearly visible.

Chapter Two: The Predator Effect

Russ Chastain, a hunting aficionado who writes on the subject of hunting, recalls an event that twenty-six years later still gives him shivers when he talks about it. He'd gone hunting with his Father. It was one of his first hunts as a teenage boy. They had set up in separate trees, and were now lying in wait for passing deer as the quiet afternoon turned to evening. "All of a sudden I heard some noises; something was moving nearby. I looked in that direction but all I could see was tree and bush moving that had been disturbed. It was still daylight."

Then, behind him, he heard rustling and saw more movement again in the bushes. "Somehow 'something' had got past me without being seen.

Then suddenly, the quiet is shattered with the most blood-curdling scream; it was the most primal cries I'd ever heard. It seemed part-human, part-animal, and part-*spirit*, and completely evil. I couldn't pin it down. It was *ethereal.* Every hair on my body rose."

"Then it came again. My heart froze, my eyes bulged in their sockets, but it was hard to pin the source down; it was ethereal and *everywhere*. I tried to shrink to invisibility. I was alone. It was getting dark," and there was something now between him and the safety of his truck.

"I held my gun tight, thinking how effective was it going to be against something from hell, something I can't see? This was freaky. Guns don't kill demons. I got out of the tree and ran."

"What was even more freaky; my Dad had not heard it!" Back at his truck, when his father returned, hours later, and asked his son where he had been, Chastain in return asked his father why he had stayed there after the screaming. His father had no idea what he was talking about − he had heard no screaming. To this day, the hunter has no idea what it was....

An anonymous contributor writes: 'My husband told me he saw something when he was in the woods the other day. He described it as being almost twenty feet with big broad shoulders, incredibly long arms, and a 'long' head. At first it was jet black. He said that it was walking in a peculiar way; that it was like it made long exaggerated strides. Then he said it became a brownish shimmering colour. He said it resembled the effects of the things in the Predator movie, but that it disappeared within thirty seconds.'

Other witnesses claim to have encountered something that has been likened to the alien in the 'Predator' movies; able to evade and elude and attack through the use of artificial cloaking, that masks its body and renders it almost invisible.

Doctor of Physics Bruce Maccabee, an expert on optics, sounds and lasers at Naval Surface Warfare Centre, and a researcher into ufo's, orbs and other unexplained anomalies describes a case of a 'Predator in the Forest,' on his site. A lady called Jan had set up a hunting stand in her native Ohio at the start of the hunting season. Sitting in the stand about fifteen feet up between the trees in a forested area, she patiently waited.

As she sat there, she passed the time texting friends and taking photos with her phone. Suddenly the woods went silent. She noticed that there was no noise at all around her; the birds had stopped, there was no rustling in the foliage. Just dead silence. It made her feel suddenly anxious and she was so unnerved by it that she sent a text saying "Something is wrong here. The woods just went dead silent...It's odd."

She thought it was possible a panther or coyote was approaching. As her eyes roamed the area, she suddenly noticed a strange visual effect that seemed to be moving across her field of vision, about twenty feet away. It looked like a mirage in a desert; but it was not hot there.

She removed her glasses and rubbed her eyes, wondering if something in her eyes was causing it. But when she put her glasses back on it was still there. It travelled from left to right in front of her, above the ground, and then eventually disappeared from sight. When it did, gradually the animal sounds of the forest returned. She later described it as 'like the invisible creature in *Predator*.'

Shortly after this, her nephew was at his High School not far away with other students. Several of them there reported seeing strange bright moving lights in the sky as it got dark. They were on their sports field, and the lights were directly above them, changing colour from white to amber, then they disappeared.

"Airplanes don't just disappear," he said, adding, "Every now and then I felt I could see something out of the corner of my eye, but it was probably my imagination."

Or was it....?

Gary Macrae wanted to explain what had happened to him after hearing me talk about a case on a radio show, that seemed to match his own. He writes; 'I was utterly shocked that this is going on all over, I had no idea. I have to say that this makes my own sighting even more frightening, as I can no longer brush it off as imagination, although dogs don't imagine things.'

'I am giving you permission to use my story, if you so wish. I can also confirm that I am college educated and, until recently when I became ill, I was a software engineer for 25 plus years. I'm not mentally ill, as some may suggest and neither is my university educated wife.'

What had happened to Gary you may wonder? Well, "I live in Kirriemuir, Scotland, which is on the edge of the Cairngorms National Park. Please take the time to read this as I think it may be of great interest and you will actually see what I saw. I read a couple of your books on holiday and was fascinated, as there seemed to be a link to several terrifying experiences I had 2-3 years ago. These were not imagination; my wife was involved also and my dogs went ballistic at the entity we saw. Let me explain.'

'Around 4 years ago, I was walking my dogs at night, in the winter on a moon-lit farm track half a mile outside of Kirrimuir. I had a torch but did not have it on due to it being a clear moon-lit evening. To the left of the road, fields drop off sharply towards a small wooded area for around 200 yards. I was walking along when my dog stopped and something caught my eye.'

'I can only describe this creature/entity as something like Gollom from Lord of The Rings but almost invisible, reflecting the surroundings in the same way as the alien in the Predator films. It was taller than me, about 6-7 feet, at a guess, and it moved quickly towards the top of the hill and easily jumped a fence to end up standing crouched around 50 yards in front of me staring at me, or so it felt as I couldn't actually see the eyes. The dog was already running when I fled. I felt that it chased me but I didn't look back to find out. I ran the mile or so home, locked the doors and told my wife about it. I was pretty shaken by this and we kept it to ourselves. Let's be honest it sounds pretty ridiculous.'

'A good while passed and we had pretty much forgotten about the experiences when the most terrifying one took place. This time we were together with the two dogs, a Labrador and a Standard Poodle, which are pretty large and not easily scared, and back where I had originally sighted the entity but just on our way into the unlit area near some trees. Suddenly the dogs went apoplectic with rage and started barking like devil-dogs, looking up into a tree at the start of the farm track.'

'I shone my torch up and briefly saw the entity again, this time crouched up in the tree. The dogs were going crazy and would not go any further. We about turned and headed home. I did look back and it did not follow us into the lit area.'

'This was terrifying as we now knew that it couldn't be imagination, as the dogs had seen it. I've never seen then so crazy before that or since that. I could try to describe the fear but really, there are no words.'

'A few weeks passed and we just avoided these areas at night. My wife, Heather then had a daylight sighting. She was just outside of town in another wood one morning when she noticed everything was quiet. She again saw the shimmering shape up in the trees and immediately went home. The dogs didn't seem to notice this time but Heather was quite a bit away from where it was. She didn't go back there alone for a long time afterwards.

'A few months later I was walking my Labrador in the Kirriemuir Den, which is a large un-lit park in the middle of the town. It is like a small valley with trees at the top and bushes dotted around. Again, it was a moonlit night but I was using a torch because it is very dark in there. I was walking along and had a feeling that I was being watched and the dog seemed uneasy.'

'It all came back to me and I started to sweep the torch around the hillside hoping that nothing was there, but it was running down the hill at an angle towards me, it turned away from me when I shone the CREE torch on it. The torch I use is one of those very powerful night fire models and I saw it very clearly this time.'

'It did run on two legs but also was crouched forward and touched the ground with it's very long arms as it moved. It was definitely the same thing. Around 6-7 feet tall, humanoid, but spindly like Gollum. Reflecting its surroundings. The torch shone brightly off the surface of its skin. I say skin because I don't think it was wearing anything.'

'Both myself and the dog ran like hell, out of the park and into the centre of the town. Again, although it had seen me it ran away from me when I shone the torch on it. After this I did tell a few people, I have a friend whose house backs onto this park, but nobody had heard of it or seen it.'

'As an addition to this, last year one of my friends was in another wood near the town (Caddam Woods) and his Rhodesian Ridgeback dog went crazy "at nothing," in his words. It had never acted this way before and has never since. I did not tell him what I had seen before, as I didn't want to cause alarm. I did share this with my friend Alan though, the one who's house backs onto the park mentioned above.'

'The other thing I wanted to do was to send you a photo I took last year. We were in the woods, near where my wife saw the "predator" in a tree, and I felt that we were being followed. I also noticed that the dogs were keen to move on more quickly than usual. This time I saw nothing at all, I just had that feeling. It's like a shadow suddenly passes over your soul and you know something is wrong.'

'I snapped a photo behind me and later noticed this weird rectangular, translucent object to the right. I won't circle it. I'll let you see it for yourself. You will have to zoom in to the right a bit. I'm sending it to you as I don't know who to show it to. I thought that you may know someone who can make a suggestion as what it is. The photo was taken with the sun behind me without a flash. I also see something else in that box, which I pray to god is pareidolia. The something else was pointed out to me by a friend.'

'Being a surviving "prey" of the invisible predator myself, I can tell you that this is nothing from our world. To protect you, these entities cannot stand bright light. Shine a CREE torch at them if you are unlucky enough to come across one. If you have dogs then they are an early indicator that something is wrong. My dogs went apoplectic when they saw the "predator", it was up in a tree.'

'It is hard to spot. If you suspect something then stand deadly still and look around you. You can definitely see it if it moves, the effect is literally like the Predator film. Like a reflection on water or a distortion of light. Whatever I saw was roughly 6-7 ft. tall. It moved extremely fast; you cannot outrun it. Also, you can only see the shape, not the features. Never go out in the woods without a CREE torch of some sort, even in daylight. I hope that none of you ever see this. It is truly horrific. Terrifying.

'With regard to the original photo (PA160028) and the two close-ups, I fear it is not pareidolia. Something is definitely wrong there. I am not a photography expert but I do collect "vintage digital" cameras, I have around 25, and I am pretty good at telling what camera took which picture. The camera used here, an

Olympus u700, is not prone to "artefacts", so if it looks wrong then I would say it is.'

Recently I also corresponded with a man called Jeffrey. 'I'm from Parkersburg West Virginia, I hunt, fish, shoot and spend a lot of time outdoors. I really don't believe any of this crap either but last week something happened that I can't explain. On my way hunting at 6.30 am, driving on lost pavement road something crossed the road in front of me, had to be at least 15ft. tall and was a medium dark brown in colour. It glided across the road just off the ground."

"When I say crossed, I don't mean walked - it kind of glided quickly as if hovering just off the ground. It was very tall, brown and flew across the road so quickly that I really didn't see detail. All I know is, I have no idea what that was and have never seen anything like it. It was shifting rectangle in shape is best I can describe. I still can't even think what that was and I practically live in the woods."

Jeffrey gave me permission to include our conversation in this book. For those who have read any of my other books, you will have come across sightings and encounters of what seem to be shimmering, almost transluscent 'monsters' for want of a better word and the people have had the misfortune to run into them. We do no know what they are, but, just as in the case of Gary Macree, they generate a terrible sense of diquiet and fear.

Jeffrey has been a hunter all his life. He is very used to going out into the woods alone, at any hour day or night. He said, "When it happened my first and only thought was "what the hell was that" and I still can't rationalize it."

I asked him, did it have any substance to it or could you see right through it? "Yes, it was a shifting dark brown shape that hovered quickly across the road. If you have ever seen a flock of birds tightly grouped together it moved like that. You could not see through it. It had a shape and I don't think my mind even accepted what I saw. It scared the hell out of me then. I thought that couldn't be real and tried to dismiss it. Does that make any sense?"

"Yes, it does, though what it was I do not know. But I have found other people who have had similar experiences. Almost as though something was shifting in density." I asked him, "Was there any possible shape to it at all, in terms of any formation of a head or limbs or was it completely blurred?"

"I was expecting to see deer cross the road and when it happened I was like; "What the hell was that? That was no deer, it wasn't birds, whatever it was it was big n fast n it scared me. I don't scare easily or even believe in this kind of thing. Like I said, it happened real fast. I think my mind kind of went into a kind of shock and just couldn't accept what I just saw. All I know is it was a very large creature that hovered across the road was very fast. Never seen anything like it."

I said, "If you could make a guess - what do you think you would say it was? - or came from? do you think it was a biological entity?"

"I cannot explain and don't even know if I want to. My impression of it was it was evil."

"Do you think it was aware of your presence?"

"There is no way that was a living creature - it was too big and it moved like nothing I ever saw, yet there it was. I don't know, like I said it scared me and my first thoughts was that it was evil. Yes, it knew I was there and was in a hurry to leave."

"So it had an intelligence - to be able to know you were there - This is an impossible question I know - but, what do you think it could have been capable of doing, to you? something physical? or mental?"

"It inspired instant fear and shock to the point that you just didn't want to believe what you just saw, but after it was gone that sense of fear and terror went with it."

"Has it made you concerned when you go hunting now or have you shrugged it off?"

"I'm not one of those people that think humans can know all of what exists, it didn't harm me or even act as if it wanted to - it just was in a hurry to leave. Things exist that we can't explain. I just chalk it up to that. I'm not afraid. Just curious. You can use my name I don't care. It happened, it was a real thing, people that know me know I'm not one to be full of s.... Good luck."

A while after talking with Jeffrey, he contacted me again. He asked me, "Did you see the short video I posted on YouTube? I didn't think about it when we last spoke but the area where I sighted this "Thing" is right next to a graveyard and a very old church. This area is very isolated."

On the video he adds, "Well, this is right where I saw that thing cross the road. Right in this corner here...

this is Pleasant Hill Church established 1881 been here forever and right across is Pleasant Hill cemetery. It's pretty high here and it's pretty windy. Right down there where those pine trees are and that speed limit sign is where it crossed the road in front of me."

"It come up out of that hollow and down over to the right there its real deep back in there and there's a pond down in there but it crossed the road and went over near where that house and yard is and down through that field and disappeared real quick, so, I don't know what it was. Some people are trying to say it's the Mothman. We're 25 miles from Mount Pleasant where the Mothman is from. I don't know… guess we'll never know."

A commentator on it says; - 'If one reads about the Salem witch trials from the people who were there it was not just a case of overzealous Christians. Some of those people were mixed up in some pretty nasty dark magic. Maybe something similar happened there at some point and let something loose.'

Maybe this person has a point...

Michael Ian Black, of '*The black files*,' (michaelinablackwix) claims to have captured images of chameleon-like reptilian creatures in the Clapham Woods in Sussex, England. An area rife with rumours of decades-long occult worship, the pictures if genuine clearly show reptilian-like entities blended with the trees on which they sit. Up to six feet in length, with arms and legs and in the form of what looks like a praying mantis.

"They have the ability to blend no matter where they are; they are masters of disguise, making them almost impossible to spot."

They were not seen while taking the photos, but afterward upon looking more closely at the captured images. He claims one of the pictures shows a black shape that does not fit with the surrounding greenery. "This one has been caught before it has had time to merge with its surrounding. You can't normally see them with the naked eye."

He goes on to make an astonishing claim; "I believe this is the reason why they can abduct with ease. I believe a race of reptiles is using our forests. Clapham woods, like Rendelsham Forest has had quite a lot of UFO sightings over the years." He ponders, "balls of light" are seen in groups coming and going from woods. Are they related?

Reptiles can change their colour to match any surroundings. They could be in your house and you would not be able to see them..."

A couple of years ago, the Taiwan UFO society was sent a very strange image that had been captured by policeman Chen Yung. While hiking with friends for the weekend at Jiaming Lake in the central mountains in Tailung, he had taken some pictures. After returning home, he was looking through the photographs he'd taken when he saw something very strange. In one of the pictures was what looked like a tall half-human half-mantis type creature, just visible on the skyline.

Unsure about what it could possibly be, he sent it to the UFO society; the only place he could think might be able to help explain it. They spent twelve months analyzing the picture, having it analyzed using forensic specialists but none of them to date have been able to discredit it as a fake; nor can they say exactly what it is either. It's big, almost transparent, and appears to have webbed hands. While they all agree it's a very unusual looking creature, and not entirely human, they don't know what it is, where it comes from, or why it is here.

A report received by MUFON of an incident in February 25, 2011, was sent in by a witness who was in the Ansonia Nature centre, 150 acres of wooded hills, in Ansonia, CT. 'As I sometimes do, I was walking in the Ansonia Nature area late at night. This time, as I was on the way back through the woods, all of a sudden a deer ran frantically across in front of me, as if it had been spooked by something, and it skid and fell. I don't think it was me that spooked it. It felt like a weird quiet; like something is about to happen.'

'I walked on, taking a path on some open terrain next to the woods. While I was walking, I wasn't focusing on anything in particular, then suddenly my eyes focused on some entity approximately 25 metres ahead, crouched slightly in a very aggressive stance and staring right at me.'

'When I first saw it, it was like I already knew subjectively that it was ET of some kind. Yes, there are many other logical explanations possible, of course, but I will elaborate on the strangeness anyway, even if it wasn't extraterrestrial.'

'The figure was glowing a blue-gray. It was as though it was naked. The head was over-sized, the arms and legs were skinny. It seemed human-like in form; athletic, ready, aggressive and focused. I didn't see any eyes yet I could tell it was staring right at me and we were like two animals in the wild in a stand-off, guarding our terrain.'

'It felt as though I'd stumbled into this entity too soon, like it was waiting for me but I'd noticed it too soon and was too alert, and it turned very athletically and ran at full speed into the woods. I heard the bushes as it took off into the woods.'

'I told a friend who said it was just a person. This is very possible but there was a strange energy involved in the encounter and I had the sense I might be ambushed by it. There was an extreme sense of danger and tension. I walk in the woods at night regularly and deer approach me or stalk, and all other kinds of sounds and I don't feel scared.'

'If it had been a person, it would had to have had an eerie aura about it to scare me. And what on earth would cause him to stare at me overtly aggressively then run full speed into the woods. Crazy right? I went back the next day and looked at the exact spot. All the way along the path is very thick shrubs, trees, bushes; it's all tangled and I thought, how did it run full speed through this? It seemed impossible. It would have been impossible for me to go through it.'

'The strongest impression I get is that I felt it had been watching me, waiting for me, and I wasn't supposed to see it so soon. When it ran off, and this is very important, it was not in a scared manner but in a very confident and regimented way, and in a way that let you know it meant business and wasn't scared, but more that, it needed to get out of the area for some reason. Afterward, I was glad I went back the way I did, sure that if I had not I could have been ambushed. The feelings and impression I have is that this entity was something other than human.'

Chapter Three: Bird, Monster or Man

A witness reported an inexplicable incident to Mufon (Mutual UFO Network) in January 2014. He was driving along the Interstate 5 near the Padden Parkway overpass in Vancouver, WA, at approximately two forty-five AM, when a translucent entity over seven feet in height crossed the road in front of him.

He slammed on his breaks when the "entity" seemingly appeared in the middle of the road, out of no-where. "I saw a being hovering above the ground, about five feet off the ground. It was there in front of me in the middle of the fast lane and it was staring straight at me. It was hovering. I think it was in the process of crossing the road. All I could feel from it was extreme fear."

The witness then describes it in more detail. "It was about seven feet high, with long lanky limbs. It was about 7 feet tall. It was a human form with a smooth head yet translucent and reflecting everything around it. You could see through it but it still had a human-like form. It did not appear to be clothed. It had flaps of skin attached to the head. It did not seem to have defined features."

Then it started to move. "It took off running, but it did not run like any human or any animal I've seen. It ran with its whole body, bending and contorting repeatedly in repetitive motions, extremely fast. It ran into the bushes. It felt like everything was in slow motion, like time itself was altered."

In the autumn of 2000, twenty-five-year-old paramedic Mariusz was cycling home with his friend after spending the evening at another friend's house. They were cycling through the forested region of Koniewo in northern Poland. They'd done it many times, and this night, though it was close to midnight, the moon was full and it lit up their route. They were passing through the valley when they suddenly heard the most awful screaming.

"Terrible sounds were coming out of the forest. I couldn't compare them to anything I've heard before." Loud rumbling, moaning sounds followed; fading, them coming louder again. Then something caught his eye.

"Suddenly, a flying figure appeared at the rim of the forest, flying in our direction. My heart fell into my mouth. We stopped, perfectly still, in shock. Its face was grey. The entire figure was grey, but like a shadow. It had long hair. It seemed to have feet."

He was frozen in shock, but his friend managed to flee. Left there alone, he says; "I regretted then that I hadn't fled away with my colleague. Then I turn back, crying.

Unable to move, Mariusz watched the figure, "in sheer terror," until eventually he found the ability to move again and cycled as fast as he could away from the figure, back in the direction of his friend's house, in desperate fear that the figure was following him.

When he reached his friend's house, he insisted he could not cycle back home and his friend's mother drove both him and his friend home. "Still today when

I talk about it I feel uneasy," he tells *Truth Behind The Scenes*.

Roger Marsh has been covering MUFON's incoming cases since January 2009. Case number 83325 involves the curious witness report from a woman who was out on Lake Michigan with her husband and a group of friends, on the night of April 16th, 2017. They were celebrating one of their birthday's and they were having a great time when one of them spotted something in the sky above them

"We were about 2 miles out on the lake and I looked up and saw what looked like a giant bat. It was as tall as my husband, whose 6ft 4! It was blacker than the night sky. It was solid black, with eyes that seemed to reflect the moonlight. It circled our boat three times in total silence before heading away. It blended into the night and then was gone in seconds."

The witness also adds that five minutes later, "a bright green object was moving across the horizon. It wasn't a plane - it was bright green! And it was moving slowly. After it disappeared out of sight, we just sat there in silence, stunned

"I began to feel this overwhelming sensation of dread. I told my husband that I felt we should get off the water as quickly as possible."

Thirty minutes later, another report came in. This witness, whose case number is 83243 in MUFON records, said he was hanging out in Chicago with friends. They were all chatting outside, when suddenly; "We heard what sounded like a bird flapping its wings. One of my homies yelled like he saw a huge Lechuza!" A Lechuza is a witch, or 'bruja,' in Mexican folklore, who can turn into a giant black bird

"We walked over and saw what looked like an owl but it stood up and it was about 6ft tall! It looked right at us. It had large glowing red eyes that were completely freaking us all out."

Six days prior to this, on the 10th of April, someone else had a very unsettling encounter, also in Chicago. She contacted the 'UFO clearing house' organisation, to relate what had happened to her, although reluctant to do so, but she could make no sense of what had happened to her. She wondered if anyone could help her come to terms with what she'd faced, and explain or identify it. This report was picked up by Tobias Wayland, another member of MUFON and who runs the blog *The Singular Fortean.*

"On the street to the park (Oz Park) my dog began acting very peculiarly. She was practically being dragged as she resisted. I noticed that many of the birds you usually hear were silent. I heard the flapping of wings. I assumed it would be Canadian Geese. Then something caught my eye and what I saw scares the …. out of me still."

"I saw a large man standing there, 7 ft or taller. He was solid black, and a large pair of wings were folded behind him. These wings stood taller than the man, by at least a foot. They jutted out of his back."

"I could not see his face as it was turned away from me and perhaps didn't notice me. Then it turned and I saw bright, ruby red eyes that appeared to glow from within. It faced me. It was 7 feet tall and instead of clothes, it looked like a giant half-man half-bird. It stared at me for what felt like eternity. I felt like it could see right through me. That it could read me, that it knew what I was thinking, like it could see into my soul. It was terrifying."

"It unfurled its wings and screeched, really loud and jetted into the air. The wings were at least 10 feet from tip to tip. I do not take drugs. I know what I saw was real. I want to warn others. I never felt I was in danger – if I did not provoke it, but, I felt it could rip me apart..."

A person who read the account replied, "There are many stories of this unidentified birdman. I've also read accounts where someone climbed a mountain and found a cave they saw a big bird-like man fly to and found human bones. All I can say is I wish mainstream media would warn people to hold onto small children and pets! Many insiders on Aliens say that some of the species want to eat us and that humans wouldn't be able to handle this knowledge."

In a different forum: 'I have something really weird for y'all. This past December in Mexico it was like near 3.a.m. and I was outside around a fire keeping ourselves warm with my younger brother and my four cousins. We were just talking when we started to hear dogs barking and crying and the cows nearby started making weird noises too.'

'We didn't really worry about it, but then two red balls came out from the side of a hill. My cousin said; "It's ok; they're tractors." I asked him, "Why would there be tractors over there at 3 a.m.?" Then we remembered that our aunt had warned me not to go near there at night supposedly because the Brujas (Witches) come out. I started laughing when she told me that because it sounded so stupid to me. Well, then my younger brother says, what if they are Brujas and we all stop talking. Then my cousin says, "What if they see the fire...?" And we all take off running into the house because we see one of the red balls getting closer.'

'We get inside and close the door. We were like "Wtf was that...?" And then all of sudden someone or something is trying to open the door violently. My little brother runs to my mom's room and tells her. She comes out and the door is still trying to get open. Then my mom walks towards the door and it goes away.'

'Next day we went to the hill to see what was there... and there was this black doll standing up. I never went back to that hill after that. We saw many red balls during those two weeks in Mexico. They would move back and forth and back and forth...it was crazy... I also a UFO. Oh...and one night when I was outside I was closing the gate and someone was saying my name close to my ear (But I was by myself!!) It sounded like a girl's voice...I don't know if y'all are going to believe me because it sounds stupid but man, I take it serious now.'

Chapter Four: Giants Monstrous?

Husband and wife, Neil and Sally Pike were keen UFO watchers. Neil was a bank employee, while his wife was the daughter of a former chief detective in the Wiltshire Constabulary. Neither were prone to drama nor fantasy. They often went out to the hills in Warminster, Wiltshire, England, to see if they could spot any flying objects in the skies above them. On August 22nd, 1972, at 10 p.m. on Cradle Hill, Mr. and Mrs. Pike were standing by the White Gate when their attention was drawn to the hawthorn tree on the military side of the fields. (The Military own a large part of the land there.)

From behind this tree came a sound as though from some large animal – the first to come to mind was that it was a cow that was trapped and struggling to free itself. Mr. Pike shone his torch around the area. There were no visible movements although this sound continued, then suddenly the sound took the form of "deliberate heavy footsteps crashing through the cornfield nearby, and coming on to the roadway."

At this point both Mr. and Mrs. Pike were feeling a terrible sensation of fear. Sweat poured from Mr. Pike's forehead and Mrs. Pike's whole body trembled. Someone or something was approaching them but nothing was visible. Mrs. Pike's nerve broke and she ran to their car close-by.

Just before Mr. pike followed her, he heard sounds accompanying the footsteps - heavy breathing. He didn't stop to hear anymore but fled from the hill, convinced that something undoubtedly evil was present on the hill that night. This was not their first experience. One winter night the year before, Mrs. Pike was at the top of a hill keeping watch while her husband was at a location a short distance away from her, also keeping a look-out.

The area at the time had been having all kinds of strange reports about unknown phenomenon, and the media was often reporting about peculiarities in the area, including local journalist Arthur Shuttlewood.

As the night drew on, Mrs. Pike was getting ready to call an end to the evenings uneventful hours, when she suddenly started to feel very nervous for no reason. Then she caught something out of the corner of her eye. Turning her head toward it she saw the clear outline of a figure coming toward her. The moon lit up the figure and she could see that it had the shape of a man, at least seven feet tall, but his arms were almost of an equal length and hung loosely at its sides. It seemed to have no neck; his head seemed to rise straight from the shoulders, with no neck....

Meanwhile, her husband was over near an old deserted military post. As he glanced at the nearby path leading up to the post, he suddenly saw three figures of giant height. Startled, he shone his torch toward them, and in that moment the figures seemed to disintegrate into thin air; only to re-appear instantaneously in another spot close by him. Alone and confronted by these giant beings, he fled in absolute panic and terror.

Another sky watcher, a veteran named Bob Strong, had a similar experience. A glowing body of a "thing" swished down over the hill and then he heard heavy footsteps thumping. On another occasion, Shuttlewood, accompanied by several others, "Heard thumping noises coming from bushes as we walked near a barn. From the hedgerow to our left we saw three giant figures standing in a triangle at the edge of a field a distance away".

"They were eight feet tall with dome heads but no apparent necks. Their shoulders were wide and their arms were long and dangled at their sides. Although it was dark their forms were clearly discernible. We walked and the tall figures glided parallel to us....."

"All these stories, no matter how bizarre, are verifiable. All the observers will attest to them... and although incredible to our way of thinking, we must keep in mind that they represent a truly alien pattern of behaviour."

On the subject of more fully-formed monsters; The 'Flatwoods Monster' is somewhat akin to the Mothman. It was reputedly a monster that terrified and traumatised a group of both children and adults in the Flatwoods area of West Virginia, in September 1952. This group of children and adults were all out in the night-time in the Flatwoods because they had seen what they thought was either a meteor or a 'UFO' landing on the top of a near-by hill there, and they intent on going to find out what had happened.

The incident appeared to begin early in the evening, after sunset, when brothers Fred, 13 and Edward May, 12, along with their younger friend Tommy Hyer, saw a bright object in the sky, moving across it before appearing to come down in a nearby field owned by local farmer Mr. G. Fisher. The boys ran home and told their mom what they had just seen. They told her they had seen a UFO land in the farmer's field. Their mother, Kathleen Hill, accompanied by a national guardsman called Eugene Lemon, all went quickly on foot toward the spot the boys said the craft had landed.

The guardsman's dog also accompanied them, and as dogs do, it ran ahead of them and reached the spot before the group did. However, the dog returned very quickly to the group, whimpering with its tail between its legs, clearly frightened. As the group on foot reached the top of the hill where the boys said the craft had landed, they all later testified that they discovered an object amid a glowing pulsing ball of "fire." In the air, there was also a mist and a strong odour that they said burnt their eyes and noses.

It was the national guardsman who then also spotted something else. He saw two small lights by the side of the large glowing object. Shining his flashlight over at them, he saw something that caused his heart to pound. Underneath a large low-hanging tree where the small lights were, was a monster. It moved, and began coming toward him and the rest of the group, bounding toward them and from it came a shrill noise. It appeared to glide, or float, but then veered off and went toward the fire-ball.

According to the mother, Kathleen Hill, the monster was at least 10-feet-tall, and she believed it appeared to be wearing a long cloak with a hood over its head, like a monk. Its face however, was definitely not human. She described it as a round shape and with blood-red with eyes that bulged out and glowed an orange hue. They all fled in absolute terror. Almost all of them afterward were deemed to be incoherent with hysteria and shock, and vomiting.

The boy's mother contacted the Sheriff once they were home, and the Sheriff, Robert Carr carried out questioning to find out what they said had happened up on the hill. He also went to the scene of the alleged incident accompanied by the national guard. The awful odour still permeated the air but there was no monster now nor any craft or fire. The local newspapers went to the scene the next day; but nothing of the strange orb or the monstrous creature remained. All that was left were some strange tracks in the grass, and a strange unfamiliar smell.

Local Newspaper owner Mr. A. Stewart went to the site the next morning, and saw strange tracks in the mud as well as an unidentified black thick liquid on the ground. The tracks however were later assumed by some to have been caused by a pick-up truck of an inquisitive person who had also gone to look for the monster and the craft.

Interestingly, paranormal investigators a Mr. William and Ms. Smith, who belonged to the 'Civilian Saucer Investigation' group based in Los Angeles, says they interviewed a woman in her early twenties and her mother, who reported to them a very similar experience. They claimed to have had an encounter with a monster of the same appearance and accompanied by the same dreadful odour, a few days before the Flatwoods incident.

It would also appear that the young woman had to be hospitalized for 21 days due to an undefined sickness. The original group who had their encounter on the hill, were reported as suffering from sickness too; particularly the guardsman, who suffered ongoing breathing problems and severe continued vomiting. The others of the group also suffered swelling of their throats and difficulty swallowing.

The Newspapers of the day reported the encounter with the entity on the hill as "a ten-foot Frankenstein-like monster," however, they added, "State Police laughed off the reports as hysteria. They said the so-called monster had grown from 7 feet to 17 feet in 24 hours."

The guardsman however, stuck to his account that he saw a pair of bright eyes, a creature of ten feet in height, with a "blood red face." The Newspaper owner who interviewed them said, "These people were the most scared people I've ever seen. People don't make up that kind of story." "It looked worse than Frankenstein," the boy's mother said.

Most bizarre of all, one of the boys described the appearance of the monster as having "a head which resembled the ace of spades, and clothing which from the waist down, hung in great folds."

Sceptics have said it was nothing more than a large owl. For the witnesses, this was an impossibility to even begin to agree with. Even more curiously, on a forum discussing this 'monster,' are two very similar accounts, but with a wholly different interpretation....

Chapter Five: Monsters in the Woods

"I made some 'Whoop' sounds while fishing, just joking around. Then something intimidating came crashing through the trees, breaking branches as it came," says Scott Carpenter. "That began my fascination with bigfoot, and studying the existence of it, particularly in the National Parks."

He believes he's had another encounter; only this time it was much closer and he claims the creature was 'in stealth mode.' "It was squatted down. I could make out just its eyes and body shape. It was dark green; it was reflecting the foliage surrounding it." He didn't see this at the time; he discovered it when watching back the video he'd recorded as he'd walked through the woods. "After walking past it, it turns back to black; that's when it comes out of the stealth mode." He posts his images online at the bf-field-journal. He says he's scrupulous at ensuring the camera is clear of smudges and debris.

Could this really be the case? It's hard to make out the images clearly, but is it equipped with these talents and if so *how* does it do it? It's certainly true that there's hundreds of reports of sightings of bigfoot that seem to vanish right in front of witnesses' eyes; to disappear into thin air in front of them, with no idea as to where it could have gone or how it has managed to disappear without any obvious hiding place.

By January 2013, the population of a Reservation in Oregon had been putting up with night after night of screeching and screaming sounds coming out of the surrounding swamps and brush. Cries, screams, and high-pitched screeching would sometimes be followed by roaring; and the combination was enough to chill everyone on the Umatilla reservation to the core.

Colleen Chance lives there and works as a housing assistant. She took to recording the sounds on her iPhone, as she was so disturbed by them. "It's spooky and I don't know what it is," she says.

According to reporter Richard Cockle of the Oregonian, she's not the only one concerned and disturbed by the nocturnal disturbances that wrecks the nerves. The housing authority has received many worried phone calls reporting the screaming and enquiring as to what on earth is causing it. Some say their dogs are too scared to venture out any more at night. Fellow housing authority worker, Mr. Luke, told Cockle, "Many here are woods people. They're familiar with animals and they're not prone to taking fright."

Witness Silva Minthorn says, "It's not the same sound as foxes; it's not even close." Her Mother believes there's more than one of them; she's heard screams coming from two different places at once, as though whatever they are, they are communicating with each other; and maybe planning something....

A woman contacted the Gulf Coast Bigfoot Research organization to describe an incident that happened to her in Connecticut. "I was riding my horse along a rail road that opens into a meadow. There's a stream there and I stopped to let my horse drink. I had a very strange feeling I was being watched and the hair on the back of my neck went up. My horse was looking at a hill and was very anxious. A smell came. It was foul. Then something started down the hill after us. It sounded like an elephant charging and its screams were so loud it hurt. I could hear branches being snapped. The horse bolted but I managed to stay on. It kept pace with us on the other side of a stone wall. I was beyond terrified. I finally started to breathe again after we got back on the road, but my horse never recovered and it died a month later."

The Toronto Sun reported on the day Helen Paphasay and her Mom got the fright of their lives. As they were driving to a blueberry site to go picking, just off the Grassy Narrows First Nation reserve, they were suddenly confronted by an unnerving sight.

"I seen a tall black thing walking toward us," she recalls. "I know it wasn't an animal because it was walking upright, walking like we walk; human-like. It wasn't an animal. It looked about 8 feet tall; black as night."

Her mother saw it too and she sat rubbing her eyes in sheer disbelief at first; then fear took over them both and they drove away from it fast. When they reached home they told the rest of their family, who were so intrigued by their story that they insisted they go back with them to try to see it too. With strength in numbers, they all went back to the same spot. What they discovered there was highly strange; they found footprints in the woods. The footprints, nearly 16 inches long, showed the outline of not five but six toes.

Similar to this Mother and daughter account, CBC News carried an eyewitness report from 2012 where two friends had also gone berry picking, in Nunavik, Quebec. As they gathered the berries amongst the trees, they thought they spotted another person close-by also picking berries. They saw her long dark hair. Then they realized the hair carried on past the 'person's' head; it covered their entire body.

As they watched in horror, they saw 'it' start to walk upright with incredibly long strides, then sometimes crawl along. It was coming their way. "It wasn't a human," says Maggie Cruikshank, "we weren't sure what it was at first, but it was really tall and it kept coming toward us, and then we could tell it definitely wasn't human."

She estimated it was between 10-15 feet tall, and that's definitely not human. They were too frightened of what it might do to them to let it get any closer, and they ran to their ATV and raced away in terror. They went straight back home to warn everyone of what was roaming out there. Footprints later discovered in the area where it had been, were over 40 centimeters long; that's nearly 16 inches. The average length of a man's foot is 27 centimeters; that's just over 10 inches.

On March 4, 2014 on Vancouver Island in British Columbia, a Marine officer had a shocking sighting. Luke Swan, a young First Nations man says he was on routine patrol at White Port beach, when standing on the shore line he suddenly saw a large dark figure perched on a near-by rock. Then it stood up.

"The first thing in my mind was to get off that beach," he laughs, telling CTV News. "I pushed off as fast as I could and got into the deep water. Something really big was standing there. It was huge. It was eight to nine feet tall. It had broad shoulders.

When I saw it scared me. It was no bear. Probably a lot of people want to see it, but in the end it might scare them too and I don't wish that on anybody. It's definitely out there," he says, not able to define what 'it' is, but definitely not keen to encounter it again. After telling his father what had happened, his father and friends went to the spot where Luke had seen the creature and attempted to track it.

They came across footprints that were sixteen inches long and eight inches wide. They spotted bark pulled off a cedar tree at a height of over nine feet. Thought they didn't see the creature itself again, Luke has no doubts he saw it.

In Chatham, Massachusetts, the police were called by Michael Patrick and his mother in 2011, after enduring night after night of screeching and screaming noises. Then they came across an unusually large footprint in their back garden. "My neighbour's dog won't leave its owners side at all now. It had gone outside to investigate the other night, after they had heard the screams too and been disturbed."

The police department told the State Journal Newspaper that an officer had seen the footprint and it was over eighteen inches long. It had claw marks. The footprint was found beneath an apple tree, and apples had been taken from the highest branches. Local investigator Stan Courtney says that a headless rabbit found beside the house could well have been left by the creature as an offering or 'gift.' He says this is often the habit of these large beasts. "Its head had been pulled off; not cut or bitten, but actually pulled off."

Whatever did it, it was strong....

Sightings are coming again in Gideon, Oklahoma, according to residents there. The sounds of thudding footsteps coming, the ground shaking beneath them. Cheryl Mast knows it wasn't her imagination when something loud thudded against her trailer in the night. With the nearest neighbours several miles away, her and her boyfriend and their friend in the trailer next door are pretty isolated. "My dog was crying and something had broken the door of the pen. I think it threw the dog. My friend is certain something shook his trailer. Her whole trailer has been shaken. It went on for several minutes. It's happened before," she tells Taklequah news. "We are scared to death," she says. "There's that feeling it's watching you. With so many incidents it makes me think we're getting close to a confrontation."

Sasquatch contactee and researcher Keegan Reid says that dogmen also inhabit the forests and woods. 'Sometimes you might just see them. Other times they may attack us – if we're out there with guns, whether it's dogman or the sasquatch people. Anubus was a dog-headed being that guarded the portal to hades, in the lower vibrational realm. That's what dogman does – they will sometimes be seen with Sasquatch but, dogman has been known to kill Sasquatch people.'

'There's 4 different types of Dogmen – there's one called the Beast of Seven Shoots – a baboon face dogman creature that stands about 20 feet height. They reside in high mountainous areas – the Appalachian mountain range has a lot of them but any mountain range will have them. You have the lycanthropes, (the were-wolf types). The skinwalkers - a lot of the time they are from indigenous people. They have taken the right-hand path like a black witch – these are shamanic traditions. They have chosen the darker path among the Dogmen for whatever reason, because these Dogmen have something to do with the lower realms.'

'Another form of dogman looks like the Vitruvian man – looks like our body type with the dog head. Another type is like the sasquatch but they have hook legs like the dog. Scott Carpenter, who was a bigfoot researcher, he got out of it 'cos he saw Sasquatch being killed by a Dogman. It freaked him out 'cos the Dogman ripped the sasquatch person's head off in front of him. It just ripped his head off – scared the hell out of Carpenter. Now there's another type that may have worked with the US Government and they're a shorter type – 4-5 feet tall, usually black in colour and they have the head and body shape of a German Shepherd. They're mercantiles – traders. They trade goods. They can go from corporeal form to post-plasma form.

What have the US government been using them for?
And, what exactly are they trading? And, with who?

Chapter Six: The Skinwalkers

'Navajo_Joe' relates his story: 'I was a kid when this happened. My uncle and I were finishing up gathering firewood because it was getting dark. Driving back on the dirt road I had this awful sense of being watched.'

'Before I could turn to look out my passenger window, my uncle shouted; "Don't!" I froze. I heard a 'tap-tap' on my window. My heart felt like it was beating out of my chest. My uncle sped up and began praying in my native language. I didn't know what was going on, but I thought it was all over – until our truck suddenly dipped.'

'My uncle began saying; "Look at me! Don't turn away!" over and over again. Then I heard it again; 'tap-tap,' but this time it was coming from the window behind me! It was getting harder for me to breathe. I wanted to cry.'

'A minute or so passed and the truck dipped again. My uncle looked around and sighed. It was quiet. "We will ask your father to do a prayer so the evil will forget our faces," he said. I remember curling up on the seat and just staring, my uncle singing an old prayer until we got home.'

In 2005 a post appeared on SG Forum. It described the experience of a young lady. All of her life, Frances T. says she has seen things, and heard things. She was born into a family of sensitives, and accepted that this was 'normal' for her. However, nothing could have prepared her for what they encountered one dark night on a remote and desolate road in Arizona 20 years ago. The family had moved to Flagstaff, Arizona in 1978 shortly after she had graduated high school. Not long after this, the family decided to go on a road trip back to their home county in Wyoming in the family pickup truck, to visit friends. Route 163 took them through the Monument Valley Navajo Tribal Park on the Navajo Reservation. "My friend, a Navajo, warned us of traveling through the reservation, especially at night."

The trip was uneventful. But their return journey more than justified the warning. "To this day, I have major anxiety attacks when I have to travel through the north country at night. I avoid it at all costs."

It was about 10:00 p.m. that night when the family were heading back. It was a long stretch of road and so pitch black they could only see a few feet beyond the headlights on that moonless night.

Her father was driving, with she and her mom in the cab beside him and her brother in the back of the pickup. Suddenly, her father broke the silence. "We have company."

She and her mom turned to look out the back window. Headlights appeared over the crest of a hill, then disappeared as the car went down, then reappeared. Thunder began in the distance and her father decided her brother should come inside. She opened the slider window and her brother crawled in. The car was still behind them.

She watched as the car's headlights crest another hill. It didn't reappear. She kept watching, turning every couple of minutes but never saw them reappear.

When she turned one last time, the truck was rounding a tight corner in the road, and her father slowed the truck. From that moment, the atmosphere changed somehow. Time itself almost seemed to stop.

Her mother screamed, while her father cried out "Jesus! What the hell is that!?"

She had no idea what was happening. Her brother was now yelling "What is it? What is it?" Her father immediately flipped on the inside light, and she could see he was petrified. "I have never seen my father that scared in my life. He was white as a sheet."

Panic was filling the cab. Her mother was wringing her hands. Her brother just kept saying "Oh my God! Oh my God!"

As the pickup sped round the corner, her father hit the brakes to stop the truck from going into the ditch. Something leaped out of the ditch. It was black, hairy and was at eye-level to them. If it was a man it was like no man she had ever seen.

Despite its monstrous appearance, whatever it was, it wore man's clothes. "It had a blue and white checked shirt and I think jeans. Its arms were raised up over its head. Its eyes were yellow and its mouth was open."

Although time seemed frozen in this moment of horror, it was over within a few minutes as the cab raced away from the thing. The car that had been following them never did show up. They drove all the way home with the interior lights on.

However, that was not the end of it. Just a couple of nights later, she and her brother were woken by what sounded like drumming. Quickly they looked out the bedroom window into their backyard, which was surrounded by a tall fence and forest behind it.

At first, they saw nothing but the forest. Then the sound of drumming got louder, and they saw a group of "men" appear behind the fence. It looked like they were trying to scale the fence to climb over, but they couldn't manage to climb it as it was so high. They began to chant.

A few days later she asked a Navajo friend about that strange and frightening night. The friend told her it was a Skinwalker that night on the road and she added that that the 'men' who had come to her house and began chanting had been skinwalkers too, and that they wanted her family, but could not gain access because something was protecting them.

"Your family has a lot of power," the Navajo friend said, "and they wanted it."

Next comes a chilling tale of abductions, mutilations, murders of adults and children, time slips and sorcery, and it ended in 'the world's last witch-trial.' It took place in 1880 on a remote Chilean island called Chiloe and was said to have been carried out in the name of 'La Provincia Recta', translated as the 'Righteous Province.' This was the term given to the rulers there; a sect of warlocks who lived in a hidden cavern.

Gruesomely, these warlocks were said to take to the sky and fly around the Island wearing magickal 'clothing' which was made from the flayed skin of their deceased victims.

Lying close to the 35th parallel, the island has a mysterious and sinister history. It was the spot in which at the beginning of the 16th century the Inca Empire ended, and according to the Smithsonian, 'a strange and unknown world began.'

A place of rain and cold and untamed forests, to the Incas, it was a place where the Warlocks lived and evil came from. English travel writer Bruce Chatwin unveiled the history of the Warlocks to the world, describing them as male witches, "who existed for the sole purpose of hunting people." According to their own testimonies at their trial, they ran protection rackets on the island, and would dispose of their enemies by sajaduras: that is, by magically inflicting cuts to the flesh.

Their headquarters was located in a cave, the entrance of which had been camouflaged to maintain its secret existence. It was lit with torches fueled by the burning of fat from their victims' bodies. The warlocks and other witnesses swore at the trial that the cave was guarded by two monsters who ensured that no-one could enter and seize the secret treasures they kept there, including an ancient leather spell-book and a bowl, which when filled with water was said to allow secrets to be seen in it.

Mateo Coñuecar was one of the Warlocks who gave testimony, and he described his first time visiting the secret cave when he was a young initiate. He said that he had been ordered to go to the cave to feed the 'creatures' inside of it. He went with another Warlock, who, when they approached the destination of the cave, began to dance ritualistically in order to open the cave entrance. He used a "special alchemy key," to open it, and the layer of earth hiding it came away.

Two disfigured entities burst out of the darkness at them. One he described as looking like a 'goat, which dragged itself on four legs.' The other was a naked man. The man was an 'invunche;' a deformed man who had been abducted as a baby and taken to the cave to become its guardian.

After being taken from its home and brought to the cave, according to Chatwin, its arms, legs, hands and feet were purposely dislocated. Then the warlocks got to work on its head. This was a slow and methodical task whereby each day, the baby's head was twisted a tiny fraction more than the day before so that eventually it was rotated by a full 180 degree and the child could look straight down the line of its own spine.

Chatwin continues, "Once the child is able to do this, the final adaptation is done. On the night of a full moon, the child is laid prostrate and tied down and its head covered over. A 'specialist' then takes a sharp knife and cuts a deep hole under the right shoulder blade. Into this hole he places the child's right arm and then sows up the hole. The child has now become the cave guardian; the 'invunche.' It is kept in the cave forever and fed with human flesh. It never learns to speak nor read or write. It responds only with guttural noises.

The tiny populace of the Island were terrified of the Warlocks and their supernatural powers. The Warlocks claimed they would fly at night, in the human skin they wore which glowed with shiny phosphorescence from the grease of the skin. They claimed they could turn themselves into any animal, being 'Shape-shifters.' They could magically transport themselves to a 'Caleuche,' a ghost ship. It was a glowing ship that today is still seen by islanders. Many of them believe that the ship is a harvester of souls.

In order to become one of the Warlocks, an initiate must wash away their sins in the freezing sea for night after night and then prove they are cleansed of all human emotions and feelings by killing a member of their own family.

It was claimed that once they had passed their initiation, the secret sect would then celebrate their new member joining, by feasting on the roasted flesh of a new-born.

According to the warlock named earlier, he carried out 'hits' for payment. When a woman on the island went to him because her husband had been seduced by another woman, he killed the love rival for payment of not money, but cloth.

Since the times of the witch trials, Chiloe has lost none of its mystery. It's said to be a place where it's almost as though a parallel universe exists with it or alongside it, for there have been many unexplained disappearances and bizarre events. Steeped in mythology and folklore, there have been sightings of a variety of odd creatures, including the 'brujos;'

shape-shifters who are immortal and who can take the form of wolves, fish, or humans. They can even take the form of rocks. It has been said that when they take the form of a human they are always very tall, and blonde. Sightings of these beings go back to before the time of Columbus yet there were no Caucasian blond races in South America before Christopher Columbus. It's these Nordic looking humans who are said by the inhabitants to be behind the disappearances of people on the Island.

Along with the Nordic sightings are the reports of the Ghost ship, the Caleuche, which again is reported to be able to shape-shift. When described, it bears striking similarities to UFO sightings in terms of appearance, and those who have seen it have also often reported incidents of missing time and relocation from where they last were. Some have described it as without doubt a ship, while others have said it has glowing lights, and yet other witnesses talk of strange glowing rocks or trees. Along with the sightings are usually the simultaneous reports of the most beautiful and ethereal sound of music. Those who have the sighting are often abducted; those who do not see it but hear the music have been reported to have become deranged as a result.

The Chilean newspapers have reported on cases of young men who have disappeared as youths, never to be seen again until decades later when they have reappeared as old men. One such case was reported by the journalist Antonio Cardenas Tabies, who spent many years obsessed by the strange accounts he kept hearing. In his book, 'Boarding the Caleuche,' he collected more than 50 testimonies of local islanders in the 1970's; all of varying ages and backgrounds. One man he interviewed as a boy of 16 had gone fishing alone one day when he suddenly disappeared.

Two days later he was found alone and wandering aimlessly along the beach on the Island.

He seemed to be in a complete daze when he was found, and when he was asked where he'd been, he said that when he got to a small hill that overlooked the ocean he began to hear a strange hum, like the sound of a generator running; but he said it was more like two generators running together at the same time. That was the last thing he could remember until he was found on the beach two days later. When he was taken back to his home, his family were very concerned when they saw that under his shirt he had a large scar that he had not had before. It was a huge scar that was shaped like a hand with long thin fingers.

When they asked him how he had got it, he could not remember and he said that he didn't recall having been in any pain. Even stranger, the scar looked like it had been there a long time, not like it was a fresh wound. Antonio Tabies returned to interview the same man five decades later, when he was by then in his sixties. The grown man was reluctant to be interviewed again, and when asked about the scar he said that he could not reveal how he had got it or he would die.

The reason for Antonio's own obsession with interviewing people was that he too had a similar inexplicable incident when he was growing up, of missing time and then being 'returned' to the Island changed.

Chapter Seven: Men, Monsters, or Shifters

Stories of a creature known as an Aswang are especially common in Malaysia and the Philippines, where it seems to specifically target the vulnerable; the elderly, infants, and the sick.

Stories abound of them attacking people, kidnapping people, and even robbing graves to eat the dead bodies. They have been described as appearing like a vampire, a witch, or a range of terrifying mythical-like beasts. It seems that they can shape-shift at will; they can appear in the form of a beast or as a human. It's believed they are cannibals of both the living and the dead.

Xiao Qian writes on True Pinoy ghost stories, "My grandfather was suffering due to age, and we were just waiting for his last days. Those last few days were the most terrifying and hair raising of my life. My family were all awake attending to my grandfather, bathing him and feeding him and so on.

Suddenly a smell like a rotting cadaver came. It gave us a feeling of panic. Then came a strange sound; like a huge bird. It was so loud, and it was screeching. Then something landed on the roof. Its shadow could be seen on the neighbour's house. The sound it made petrified us; it was scratching on the roof and it sounded like metal being torn apart.

Our servant boy went outside to look and started screaming, "There's a big black thing; its eyes are bloodshot red!" The family huddled together in fear until finally the thing departed, moving on to terrorize another family before it would choose its next victim.

Micha F. Lindemans, of Encyclopedia Mythica says, 'I have had a real experience of this monster. At the time, I was a boy. We lived in a small village surrounded by trees. That night I couldn't sleep as the neighbour's dogs kept howling and I opened the window to look outside. The moon was very bright and I saw the dogs. Then I saw something else, something dark floating horizontally in front of my neighbour's window. It looked like a person floating. I was very scared and I quickly closed my window and covered myself with my pillow. The next day I talked to my neighbour. I asked him if anything happened last night. He said he and his sisters and brothers were trying to guard their Mom because there was an Aswang.'

It's said that the Aswang can enter a person's body; and when they have done this, they use that person to inflict terror and great harm on their enemies. Most usual are the female Aswang, who in their own form will appear to witnesses as unsightly with dirty long mated hair, evil blood-shot eyes, long sharp nails, and a long black tongue. Like the traditional witch, she allegedly has the power of flight, and she may then transform into a huge bird to hunt her prey.

According to author and occultist Jimmy Lee Shreeve, one instance of a shape-shifting entity was even a matter of a murder trial in South Africa in 1987. Zane Metshiavha was suddenly woken in the night by strange scratching noises at his front door. He went to the door and called out, asking who was there. When he got no response, he became scared and to protect himself he went and fetched an axe. More confident now that he had something to protect himself with, he opened the front door and went outside. To his horror he saw what looked to be large bat hanging from the rafters of his roof. He struck it with the axe, making it fall to the ground and then he fled in blind panic.

He went to his neighbours for reinforcement and having roused several of them he returned to his yard with them. These witnesses later described seeing the creature dragging itself across the yard toward a fence. Zane struck it again and again until it lay still. The group of people watching him approached it to look at it more closely.

Each of the witnesses described it in a different way when they spoke in court. Some of them described it as looking like a mule, others said it was definitely a winged creature; but all of them stated that the creature's form was changing shape before their eyes. They watched it changing. All the testimonies stated that began to form into the body of a child, and then into a fully formed man.

After it died from the injuries sustained from the axe, it was identified as that of an elderly man, Jim Nephalama, who was reputed to be a wizard. The villagers said he would often tell people that he had "the power to do whatever he wished with them." He would boast that no-one had as much power as he, and he warned his enemies that his battled were not fought in the day time but at night. He was feared by all who encountered him.

When the case went to the Supreme Court, the judge ruled that Zane should have recognized that the creature was a man. He was found guilty of behaving in an irresponsible and violent manner and sentenced to ten years in prison for culpable homicide. On appeal, and further witness testimony, the sentence was later reduced to four years.

Chapter Eight: The Hidebehind & The Bunyip

Does a creature known only as 'The Hidebehind' really exist? Allegedly a fearsome creature that preys upon unwitting hunters and hikers who wander into the woods, it was certainly credited as the cause of the disappearances of some of the early loggers who worked in rural regions.

When they never came back to camp at the end of a hard day, it was said they had been taken by the hidebehind. Its success is said to lie in its inherent ability to become unseen; hiding behind trees when stalking unsuspecting victims and snatches them away in the blink of an eye.

The hidebehind are not the only ones who play this game. Could it be true that a cannibalistic humanoid lurks in the beautiful wilds of New Zealand? According to Maori legends, the fearsome Maero are a race who live in the woods and mountains. They are masters at snatching people in the wilderness. They steal people away and then fight them to their death. Wild, hairy and exceptionally ruthless, these Maero leave no one alive. Once dead, they feast on the bodies.

The Maero, also sometimes called Mohoao, have hair that's long and unkempt, all over their bodies, and long cruel fingers. One story tells of a man called Tukoio who was once captured by a Maero. He fought with the savage creature and managed to overcome him. He chopped off the beast's head and decided to carry it back to his village to show off his trophy, but as he began to walk along with it, to his horror, it began to talk to him. He threw it to the ground in shock and fled.

Later, fortified by some villagers accompanying him, he returned to where he'd dropped the head. It was gone….. The Maero had reassembled its head onto its body and back to life to terrorize and kill and eat more villagers.

In the 1800's, New Zealand's Governor, Sir George Grey, said he had been told about this 'creature' by the islanders: "They say they're like a man but covered with hair, with long claws; strong and active, and they say they are afraid of them."

It was indeed reported that a headless partly eaten body of a gold miner was found in 1882, followed by the dead body of a woman just a short distance away, who had been dragged from her shack in the night. Her neck had been snapped….

Now to the Bunyip: In Mulgildie. Australia, it is here that local people from successive generations claim that the Bunyip lurk. The bunyip are said to lurk in swamps, creeks, riverbeds, and waterholes. Exactly what the bunyip is however, has never been entirely established. The word 'bunyip' is translated from the Aboriginal dialect as meaning "devil,' or "evil spirit." From as far back as 19th century accounts of this 'being,' descriptions include those of a strange creature with a dog-like face. It was said to be "11 paces long" and "4 paces in breadth."

The legend of the bunyip has lived long in Australian history. With Aboriginal Elders and generations of farmers having told tales about the eerie sensation of hearing the sound of bubbling water, and of their cattle then mysteriously disappearing. Residents in this small township of Mulgildie say they have a waterhole where the bunyip live. 'The Bunyip Hole' is a still pool covered in green slime, and it is known to gurgle. The belief is that this hole is connected to an underground waterway network. Local woman Joan Farrell moved to the area in 1970's and she told reporters, "You don't go there, especially in the dark, and you don't swim in it, because you can get dragged down never to be seen again."

The problem is no-one really knows what one looks like exactly; Part crocodile, part-dinosaur, with a dog-like head, or more like a bird's head. Dark fur, facial horns and a bulky physique. The size of a cow. An aggressive animal with supernatural powers. It is said to lurk in billabongs and rivers awaiting its next meal and according to Aboriginal legend, that meal is sometimes human. It warns its victims of their imminent doom with a terrifying howl. Is this just superstition? The Sydney Morning Herald on January 4th 1947, wrote of the curious case of the "Wailing at the Waterhole."

Staff writer Bill Beatty said, "Various theories and conjectures can be offered, but not substantiated, regarding the terrifying screams that come from the Watering Hole over so many years." The Waterhole lies on the way to Isisford, in Central-Western Queensland. He continues; "The records of this uncanny phenomenon are many. It is said that the noises were first heard more than 8 decades ago. It was said by bushmen to be the bunyip. Inevitably, controversy began as to whether there was such a creature, and yet even it was never credited with emitting such blood-curdling screams as those that came from the Watering Hole."

"The many stories are consistent and they always feature a series of terrifying, fiendish yells and screams, that arise suddenly and then die away mysteriously into silence. On record is the account from more than 50 years ago when two shearers, on their way to a station, had camped up by this water-hole on a warm summer evening. The hole was well supplied with water, and after leaving their horses to graze, the two men made tea over their fire, ate dinner, and yarned for a few hours. The fire had nearly died down, and the men yawning, when suddenly there came a soft, distant wailing that grew rapidly nearer and louder.

To the astonishment of the two men, the cries appeared to be in different keys; devilish, unearthly shrieking, such as no human voices have ever uttered. The screaming was now ringing in the men's ears at a deafening pitch, and it was coming from the waterhole. They thought their ear-drums would surely burst, yet they were too terrified to move.

Then, to their fervent relief, the shrieking diminished in volume until it was merely a weird wailing. Moments later, it ceased completely, and all was a deathly silence. Throughout it all, not a ripple came across the surface of the water from which the noises had come.

The men quickly caught their horses and rode off. When the men told their story later at the shearing station, it was received with derision by some, but others there told of it being a notorious spot. They told of instances where cattle had arrived there exhausted, but had stampeded as the sun went down.

The Newspaper continues with another story about a new farmhand who had just been employed at a nearby Station. He had brought his wife with him and they had settled to live in a hut he built by himself near the Watering Hole. She had lived in the outback all her life, and was used to the harsh living and the isolation when her husband was away working long days and nights on the Station. However, they had only been living there a few days when he came home late one night and found his wife in a state of hysteria and near-collapse. She could describe nothing she had seen but had heard the most awful shrieking noises, which seemed to have come from the Watering Hole.

Her husband said that it must have been some nocturnal birds. Unfortunately, he was away for two nights soon after this, and on his return, he was confronted by the terrible sight of his wife almost having lost her mind. She told him that she had heard the most horrifying screaming and wailing coming from the water. Fearing for her very sanity, her husband took her away from there that very night and they never returned.

On hearing of this incident, at the Station where he worked, a few of the men decided to go down to the Watering Hole and camp out for the night to brave the unknown. They were careful to ensure that they could not be made victims of a practical joke, by placing scouts at posts around them, to ensure no-one crept around down there and spooked them. They sat around the roaring fire swopping stories and smoking until after midnight, when they settled into their blankets. It started as a soft low wail. By the time they had got to their feet it had reached screaming pitch, of a sound each of them knew was not uttered by bird, beast, or human. They fled as fast as they could and none would ever return there again....

Chapter Nine: The Wendigo

Does a ghoulish man-eating monster called The Wendigo really exist? Taller and larger than a human, with fangs and a grotesque face, such a creature has been spoken of by generations of Native Americans, and 'The Wendigo' is translated as meaning: "An evil spirit who devours men."

It was believed to be a terrifyingly real entity by First Nations tribes. When 17th century missionaries and explorer came, they at first ridiculed the accounts of such a creature existing; until they themselves began to experience their own threatening and horrifying encounters.

They described coming across a strange and terrifying beast they could only describe as 'the Devil himself,' or 'a Werewolf,' because of its fangs and glowing eyes. The Wendigo is described by scholar Basil Johnston as "gaunt to the point of emaciation, its desiccated skin pulled taut over its bones, which push out against the skin. Its complexion is of ash, the ash-gray of death, and its eyes, deep in its sockets. It looks like a skeleton disinterred from the grave. Its lips are tattered and bloody."

Wendigo's are believed to be cannibal creatures of supernatural lore, who will consume people yet never become satiated. The taste of flesh would merely provoke even greater hunger in them and they would fly at night with wings, to hunt for their human prey.

And now we come to the tale of Swift Runner, a Cree Native American who had lived in Alberta, Canada in the last century. He was a husband and father to six children. His profession was tracker and guide for the Mounties. He was believed to have been a good father and well-liked by other members of his tribe. He traded fur with the Hudson Bay Company, and was believed to have been a trusted man.

However, that was to change when he returned from winter camp in the year of 1879. The winters there were savage; biting cold and little food and survival was a harsh business. However, he returned looking no less well and in fact, he appeared surprisingly healthy and robust. He even appeared to have put on a little weight since he had last been seen. What folks couldn't understand however, was where his wife and six children were. Upon being asked many times, and being unable to provide an answer, the Mounties were summoned and they went to the Winter camp that Swift Runner had set up, from which he had just returned. His family would surely still be there, if they had not returned with him.

However, the Mounties found only an empty camp and what looked like a grave. Swift Runner explained sadly that one of his children had died and had been buried there. The police disinterred the grave and indeed did find a pile of bones buried there. However, as they looked around the camp, they were also bewildered to come across what looked like more human bones, lying scattered. They found a skull too, which on presenting to the tracker, was told by him that it belonged to his wife; that it was her skull.

Swift Runner then sat down and began to tell the police what had happened. It began he said, when he started having dreams or rather, they were more like nightmares. He was being visited he said, by a Wendigo.

The Wendigo was gradually taking over his mind, he said, forcing him to think as they did, and to feel that hunger growing within him until he could bear it no more and he lived out his need by killing his wife in order to eat her. She was not enough though; she merely tempted his hunger to grow greater, and soon he had hung the body of his youngest son from a pole. The bones lying discarded around the camp, had been sucked dry; their marrow removed and eaten. Some of the bones had even been snapped....

Chapter Ten: Man-Wolves

Floods devastated many rural areas in the southern parts of England in the winter of 2013. Farm land and homes remained flooded for weeks on end. It was during this time that a twenty-five-year-old student, who would not reveal his name for fear of worldwide ridicule, spoke to Cryptozoology News. What he told them was far from ordinary. He said he had been on a train heading back to London, after having been to visit his parents. He'd dozed off occasionally during the lengthy journey, but when he opened his eyes, he claims he saw something completely inexplicable.

"When I woke up, I looked through the window and saw a man about nine feet tall running through the wet fields; at least, I thought it was a man...until it got closer to the train. We were moving very slowly because of the water."

"It wasn't a man. It had horns and ears like a wolf. It had hair all over its body. I don't know what it was... I thought I was still dreaming, but other passengers also saw it."

Mark Miner claims he has collected more than twenty first hand modern day accounts of what were possible werewolf sightings in Oregon State. He claims these are fully verified accounts. He's keen to stress this, obviously used to skeptical reactions.

One of those accounts is his own. "One night my fiancé and I were lying down on a deck in Montieth Park, Albany, just looking at the stars when we suddenly heard something jump in the water. We got up and looked over and something black was swimming, approximately over 7 feet long and was covered in hair. It grabbed hold of a sleeping duck and started biting into it; we could hear the crunching of its bones. We were extremely frightened as it climbed up onto the bank, but I wanted to see this 'thing' closer so I jangled my keys to attract it. It let out a growl like a dog does when you approach its food bowl when it's eating; but times that by a thousand. It was deep, guttural; its tone was the deepest anger, and it made my blood go cold. We both thought we were going to die."

"We ran and I caught a glimpse of it as I ran. It was huge and it was the wildest, most evil thing I've ever seen."

Was it a werewolf? A wolfman? One of the scariest legends in Cajun folklore is that of the Loup-garou, or rougarou. Described as a beast with the head of a wolf and the body of a man, it's thought to be an original werewolf; a shape shifting human that can transform into a wolf at will. Its natural habitat in wolf form is the thick bayou where the swamps and forestation keep it camouflaged and hidden and where unsuspecting hunters can inadvertently fall prey to its hunger and mindless slaughter of them.

Chapter Eleven: Anomalous Monstrous Creatures

Occult British scholar Richard Cavendish recorded the strange case of a Mrs. & Mrs. Smith who in 1940 were sitting together in their front room, when the wife said to her husband, "It will come over the hill when it comes; it will come over the hill when it comes."

Afterward, she had no idea what she had said, or why she had said it; despite her husband telling her, in shock and confusion, that she had said it. She did however become very scared of being in the house after it got dark. She did not repeat what she had said again, but about two months later she woke in the middle of the night and told her husband that the thing from over the hill was nearly upon them. Then they heard the downstairs door opening and heavy steps coming up the stairs. As they grabbed hold of each other in terror, their bedroom door swung open and a hideous thing came through the door.

It was bloated and naked with discolored blotchy skin. It had an odd shaped head, a thick neck, and feet that were webbed. "It was the essence of evil. Never have I experienced anything so terrible. I have never been able to find out what it was. I hope I will never experience it again," said Mrs. Smith.

It crossed the floor in front of them, went to the bedroom window and went through it somehow, vanishing without attacking them, but neither of them ever really recovered from the shock of what it was, or what it wanted with them.

The same researcher also relates the very strange case from January 1879, which occurred at night, in the area of Woodseaves, Shropshire, England. A man driving his horse and cart across a rural bridge was horrified by the sudden appearance of a black figure "with huge shining eyes" who jumped out from the tress and landed on top of the horse's back. The terrified man attempted to whip the human-shaped black form, only to find that his whip passed straight through the figure.

The horse, in a state of panic to find this bizarre creature on its back, took off in a gallop, with the black figure clinging on still to its back. At some point, the entity then vanished as quickly as it had arrived, leaving both man and horse in a terrible state of shock.

In September 2013, 120 elk were found dead in New Mexico. All were scattered near each other. Close-by was a newly formed crop circle. Had it been an infectious disease, it would have killed gradually them, not all at once. In an area rife with mysterious cattle mutilations, many are wondering if something unknown came out from the crop circle and attacked the animals. Curiously, a 1647 picture made by a method called woodcutting, called 'The Mowing Devil,' clearly depicts a demon-like creature creating a crop circle. According to the legend that inspired the picture, the circle appeared in the crop 'so neatly done that no living Man could do the like.'

Had crop circles really been appearing way back then? And how many sightings had there been of demonic creatures emerging from them?

Wallasea Island is a truly bleak marshland in Essex, England. In the 1970's English writer Eric Maple, in his book *Realm of Ghosts,* describes a disturbing incident of a beast-like creature that appeared in a barn on the Island. The barn was situated on land owned by a house that had been known as 'the Devil's House,' since as far back as the 1600's. A labourer was reported to have been at work in the barn when he heard his name called several times. After this he says that he was overcome with an overpowering, obsessive desire to kill himself, and unable to stop himself, he hurriedly grabbed hold of some rope, tied it around his neck and walked toward the ladder to scale it and secure the other end around a beam, all the while hearing a voice telling him, "Do it, do it."

Suddenly, he was confronted by the sight of a monkey-like creature staring at him with wild red eyes, which scared him so much that he ran at full speed from the barn. Locals believed the creepy experience had been due to the rumoured satanic worship that had been going on in the house, many years before.

Author Graham J McEwan collected the very strange account of a Mr. John Farrell and his girlfriend Margaret Johnson. On a warm night in 1966, they were driving on a quiet road in the rural county of Louth, Ireland. Suddenly, in front of them on the road was a creature blocking their path. At first it looked like a horse, but its face was that of a man's. Its appearance was not only extremely odd, but the menace that exuded from its eyes was terrifying. In palpable horror they both met its gaze as it loomed nearer, where it remained blocking them from going further and preventing them from escaping it.

"It had horrible eyes, they were bulging. We both screamed we were so frightened. We were completely paralyzed. It was a horse's body but the face was hairy and leering and huge. It was so big that it covered the stretch of the road entirely in front of them, before thankfully vanishing into thin air after a few minutes of silent terror. "It just *vanished*...John turned the car around and drove to my house. He drove straight through the front gate he was so frightened. We woke up my Father and told him. We weren't drunk; we didn't drink, and both of us couldn't have imagined it."

Her Father spoke to the Press some time later, saying, "They were still terrified when they arrived home. They must have seen something awful. My daughter was ill for days afterwards, and both of their stories tallied."

Chapter Twelve: The Goatmen

A lady called Heather told of her confusing and frightening encounter on Unexplained Mysteries, which happened while trekking with a friend and their horses in the boreal forests of Northern Saskatchewan, Canada.

'As the sun started to set on day one of their trek, they looked for a good place to set up camp. 'We set up the tent and realized my hat was gone; couldn't find it. Going back along the trail I found it about a hundred feet away. As I picked it up, it really stank. Anyway, we went to bed, and saddled up the next morning.'

'That night we set up another camp. At 3am I needed the bathroom. Just before I went into the trees, the same smell was back. I was nervous now, because whatever was making it must have followed us. I was scared it could have been a cougar and I grabbed my rifle. A shadow moved slowly behind a tree about fifty feet away.'

'I hummed, thinking I might hear it move so that I could figure out what it was. It echoed my humming; perfectly, gutturally. My heart started pounding; only a person could do that. The smell came back, so strong I began to heave as I made it back to the tent. My friend shouted out and started pointing the flash light, and leaves scrunched and the thing started to run; what we saw, it was dark; I might be wrong, but it looked like a man but it had an animal's head... I know what I saw.'

'The thing was the height of a man, but its legs looked like they were broken and thin. It was covered with hair. It looked distinctly human, its body was human, its arms were human, but it had a goat-shaped face... and it had horns.'

'What the hell did I see? My friend insists it must be supernatural. I have no way to explain it and I haven't slept well in days...'

As to the origin of this 'thing,' there are many theories. Some say Goatmen were created by the Nephilim; the fallen angels who procreated with women, resultantly creating a hybrid race of strange creatures; however, since its appearance is incredibly similar to that of the demonic entity Baphomet, once worshipped by the Knights Templar, and now a significant figure in Satanic worship, it's creation could well be the work of dark alchemy and sorcery. Given that they disappear without trace, and no bodies are ever found, perhaps it's more likely they are indeed inter-dimensional entities that have been summoned from hell itself.

Demonic creations that begin as mere shadows, weaker in strength until they fed off the energy of human's, taking sustenance from them to gain strength and vitality, until able to fully develop into their hideous monster-like forms. Now fully equipped, they move at lightning speed and can disappear in an instant, never to be caught or trapped, playing with human fear as though a game to them.

Margaret Zimmer of Florida MUFON describes the report she received from a man in Pennsylvania. The man, along with his brother and his son, were on a fishing trip at a reservoir. They'd made a fire to give them some lighting, as well as having a large flashlight with them. With the fire glowing behind them, they sat along the dock waiting for the fish to come.

The son was playing with the torch, flashing it behind him when caught between two trees about thirty feet away, he saw something absolutely terrifying. It was approximately eight feet tall, according to the adults present, and its arms were almost as long as its body. It was hunched over. They could not see its face. But it was definitely not a human being. Almost like an albino, it was white, and when it moved, it walked "as though its knees were on backwards..."

Chapter Thirteen: Hell Hounds

Writer Elliot O'Donnell was collecting scary ghost stories for his 1954 publication 'Dangerous Ghosts.' One night after he'd finished giving a talk in Northern England, a Mr. James McKaye came up to him to tell him about his own frightening true story.

The man said he had recently gone to view a house, wishing to move himself and his family closer to his place of work. As he was going up the stairs, he thought he could hear footsteps behind him. He turned around quickly but no-one was there. He thought how strange it was, but decided to put it down to the acoustics in an unfamiliar place.

Upstairs he went into the first bedroom. The footsteps followed him. That's when he started to get truly frightened; it was the middle of the day and it was bright inside the house. How could there possibly be a ghost in the room with him, he wondered. But then he saw the shadow on the wall, and it was not his.

It was not the shadow of anything he'd ever seen before. Petrified, he ran from the room and out of the house itself. Strangely despite this, or perhaps because of it, McKaye could not stop thinking about the house. He dreamt of it, always as a mystery which he was about to be given the answer to only to suddenly wake from the dream.

In a most bizarre decision, he applied to rent it. It was available at a remarkably low rent, which at the time he didn't think anything of; he just desperately wanted to live there.

He moved his family in immediately and all was quiet for the first few weeks until one morning when he was working in his study, and the maid came in asking him to quickly hurry to the nursery upstairs where the children were playing. "The children are playing with something like a dog, but it's not a dog. I don't know what it is," she cried.

In the nursery he saw the thing; it was a blurry outline of a form that seemed shaped like a great dog, but on seeing him it rushed from the room.

That night he was in his study after the family had all gone to bed. He was ready to call it a night and go to bed himself and as he rose to turn off the light his hand was suddenly gripped by something cold and clammy that didn't seem to have fingers. He screamed in fright and just then he heard a tremendous crash from upstairs.

Rushing up the stairs he ran into his wife's bedroom to find her talking in her sleep to something that was crouched on the floor; a black figure that looked like the shadow he had seen on his first visit to the house. It was a hideous combination of wolf and monster and human, and it emanated sheer evil, but it vanished in front of his eyes.

Within the next few hours, the family left the home, never to return there. Though McKaye did his best to find out the history of the house, he never did get to the bottom of what the creature was or why it had appeared. He did however discover that the rent was low for a reason; no-one ever stayed there long.

The infamous Hellfire Club, though founded in England in 1735, also had an isolated meeting place in old rural house at the top of Montpellier Hill, South West of Dublin. Built over an ancient sacred druid Caern, it was the scene for much debauchery and allegedly occult worship by the members of the Hellfire Club.

Reputed activities included the burning alive of black cats in black magic rituals, the murder of a dwarf, and the killing of a woman. The skeleton of the dwarf was discovered many years later under the floor along with the statue of a demon, and it was given a consecrated burial. Perhaps not surprisingly after this, there have since been many unsettling accounts of supernatural incidents and reported sightings of both black cats and huge black dogs.

Frequently visitors to the now derelict club claim to feel an ever-present sense of dread and fear when they are there; almost as if some ancient power has been harnessed and trapped within the walls of the building. Here's just a couple of many reports from those who have ventured onto the site, from Irish site *Blather.n*et; "I was there today with my friend. I'm very skeptical about these kinds of things; however, as we started going up the stairs I suddenly felt really ill. It was very strange; it just came on suddenly... and I began to think that there really is something not right about the place, and I really couldn't wait to get out of there. I felt very uncomfortable the whole time I was in there."

Domhnall O'Huigin writes, 'As a young teenager I was there with three other friends. To this day I remember the feeling that there was death in the ground, almost like an odour. That's the only way I can explain it: like someone or something had died there and there was still a sense of it all these years later that. You could ignore it but if there was a lull in conversation it returned to the forefront of your mind and felt oppressive.'

'I then went there years later with my kids, but I got exactly the same feeling; all I know is it was imperative to get my kids out of there. Make of that what you will. For the record, I am relatively credulous but do not think I am psychic or similar. I do not know what this was...'

Ciara says, 'For years my parents and me would go up there to walk our dogs. But the last time I went up there would be the last time; for a reason. 'It was the early '90's, I was about 13, and me, my mum, dad and our dog went for a walk up there. My dad was doing something fixing the car after we parked, and me and mum went on ahead with our dog. It was no different feeling to any other time I was there. It was early afternoon, sunny, me and mum were chatting and the dog was a bit ahead of us.'

'Suddenly she stopped, which made us stop. Her hackles went right up, and we looked forward and encountered this big black dog. Its eyes were black. It was snarling at us and showing its teeth. We froze not knowing what to do.... Mum told me to go back and get dad. I turned very carefully and as I looked back at my mum I saw it was gone.'

'I can't ever explain it. It had literally vanished. We ran back to my dad and tried explaining it to him, but he just thought we were being hysterical women. I've never been up there since; I don't think I could again. When I speak about it, it gives me serious chills.'

At the bottom of the hill stands Killakee House. In the '60's a Mrs. Brien bought it and turned it into tea rooms. However, the Irish Independent newspaper reported that something was very wrong there.

Spending the first few nights there alone, Mrs. O'Brien experienced some terrifying things. In the middle of the night she was woken by the sounds of her dogs howling so weirdly, "that it was as if they were frightened out of their skins."

She herself had also been terrified by strange noises, and in the mornings, she would find destruction throughout the house, yet no evidence of anyone breaking in. Workers who'd been contracted by her to carry out the renovations before opening for customers, refused to lodge in the house after witnessing unnerving incidents including a door that would not stay closed despite it being locked with a heavy bolt. One night a worker watched in horror as the door began opening and through it came a large black cat as big as a large dog. It glared menacingly at him.

Then an artist, Tom McAssy, was contracted to design paintings in the house. He was painting in the hallway when he allegedly saw a similar enormous black cat with red eyes. Oddly, he claims that the cat then spoke to him, saying, "You cannot see me." Then a hunched three-foot-tall man appeared through the door. As the painter started to back away from the apparitions, he watched in disbelief as the man himself shifted into a cat too.As though to capture the strange experience, the artist then went on to paint a portrait of the cat with a human face.

If true, it would seem that perhaps brought about by occult ritual magic, there was still shape-shifting going on in the area all these years later. With repeated nightly disturbances, the owner had no choice but to call in an exorcist. It's said that the manifestations then desisted; though reports still come from visitors to the area that it's a place where the atmosphere is filled with uncertainty, apprehension and unease. The house is now a private residence, and information about any current disturbances is not public knowledge. The Hellfire club lies in ruin, but sightings are still reported and many visitors vow never to return to the Hill.

Just around the corner from the Old Bailey Criminal Law Courts in central London, was a prison that housed people accused and convicted of serious offences, and it was here that condemned prisoners were hung in front of huge crowds of people who flocked there to watch.

Since the 16th century there has been a legend of a mysterious large black dog appearing there. Witnesses said they saw it accompanying prisoners to the scaffolds before they were hung, only for it disappear before their eyes. Others claimed they saw it climbing walls and walking along rooftops.

Prison conditions were appalling; with vermin, bitterly cold conditions, overcrowding and very little food. A highwayman imprisoned there called Hutton wrote about the black dog while he was awaiting execution. His account describes how whispered tales were told about a group of inmates who were so starving that they ganged up on a new prisoner and killed him, then ate his body.

What the gang of prisoners didn't know however, was that this new inmate was a highly educated scholar who had been schooled in the art of black magic. It was soon after his murder that the sightings of the black dog began; its appearance taunting and terrorizing those who had killed him. To this day, sightings are still reported, though the prison is no longer used.

David saw an extraordinarily large 'dog,' in 1995. He writes; 'I was on my way to my job in Freeport, Illinois. It was about 10:30pm and I was on State Road when I saw it running along the left side running near a corn field. It was keeping pace with my car. It looked at me several times.

It had black fur that was hard to focus on, like it was almost shifting. I felt it was pursuing me. It had large glowing red eyes. It was easily keeping pace with my car. I was doing 50-60 MPH. It looked at me several times. It felt very clear that it was pursuing me in particular.

At some point it turned into the field and disappeared. I do not know why I saw it, but there were other supernatural events occurring in my life at the time, so I assume it was linked somehow. I'm glad that I was in a car and not on foot; I can't imagine what would have happened otherwise....'

Chapter Fourteen: Things with Wings

Caretaker Mr. Mariella who lives in Oakland Creek, California, claimed he saw a very odd and terrifying sight one night back in October 1975. He didn't speak out about it then; he was sure people would think him crazy if he did.

Years later now, he says he recalls that as he took out the garbage that dark evening, something above him caught his eye. "It was like some fearsome gargoyle, on the edge of the roof of the house."

It was staring down at him. "It was very broad; much bigger than a man. It was monstrous. I was always afraid to tell anyone though; but it was like the devil himself."

What he didn't know at the time however, was that he wasn't the only one to encounter such a monstrous thing. Winged, gargoyle-like monsters were being seen in trees and on roof-tops throughout the area. They had massive wings, and seemed to glide silently without needing to flap their wings.

Unknown magazine, published from 1997 to early 2001, interviewed a group of youths about their strange encounter in an Illinois park. One of the boys, Ron Bogaski, told of how he and several other of his friends came face-to-face with a gargoyle.

The night it took place was in 1981, in a park on a late summer's night. They were sitting beside an old mausoleum inside the park, when suddenly they noticed an incredible sight. Sitting on the top of the gothic structure was a creature, estimated to be possibly ten feet in height, with dark leather-like skin covering it. Its body was 'very muscular with thick arms. It had enormous wings and horns on its head.'

All four of the teenagers could smell the stench of decay coming from it, along with an overpowering smell of sulphur. They watched in awe and horror as it unfurled its wings and flew up into the night sky.

Respected researcher Stan Gordon reports on the alleged sighting of a dragon-like creature seen flying in Pennsylvania, in 2012. In a rural part of town, a man was out walking his dog at close to midnight. He heard a 'whoosh,' and looked up at the night sky. Flying over him was a large thing approximately fifty feet above that looked like a mythical creature; "It looked like a dragon," the shocked man reported.

It flew over a light and the man was able to catch a better look at it. He described its body as being over twenty feet in length and with a wingspan almost as wide. It didn't have scales, but rather had a shiny, almost reflecting skin. It was coloured reddish-brown. He could see arms that were muscular and legs that were thick. Both its mouth and its eyes appeared to be glowing. The noise coming from it was deep and throaty.

On unexplained mysteries forum, a lady in her sixties now relates the experience she had as a teenager. "In 1963, I was 15, and my younger sister and I lived in Colma, California. My Mom used to send us berry picking in a wild area nearby. That day, as we started collecting the berries, I looked down the hill next to us and saw a large dark object lying there.

I was curious and climbed down to it. There was this huge dead dragon-thing. It was about 8 feet long with huge wings and claws. It was stiff. It had long sharp teeth... It was grotesque. I screamed and my sister came running. We both ran home screaming. Over the years I have found stories that say they are mythical; but I know what I saw and it was a real gargoyle. My sister and I both saw it."

Recent Gargoyles have been reported since 2010 in Puerto Rico, according to investigator Reinaldo Rios and the Guanica police. Incredibly similar eyewitness reports describe demonic looking entities of reptilian appearance, at least 6 feet in length, with leathery wings and skin, and red or yellow eyes full of intensity and menace.

A few days before, and directly after the 9/11 terror attacks in New York, witnesses and images show a huge winged entity flying from the twin towers. It seemed that Mothman had re-appeared at a scene of devastation, as it had allegedly done before; showing up at the Chernobyl nuclear disaster, and indeed at Fukashima.

Eminent researcher Colin Andrews posted a reported sighting by English businessman David Haith, who had written to him to tell him of what he had seen in 2011; prior to the Fukashima disaster. 'I was in Japan for business and staying with a friend who was teaching there. After dinner, he said he needed to see a weather project the students had created, near a power site.

'As we walked toward the small weather project, we heard a sound like a bus's brakes in need of service then a scream that made the hairs on the back of my neck stand up. A young couple nearby were staring at the power plant, and a figure was silhouetted there on top of one of the buildings. To say that this creature was large was an understatement.'

'Suddenly it unfurled a huge set of black wings and took flight, circling several times, its attention fixed on a building below; that I was to later find out were the nuclear reactors. Then it came toward us. It had two large eyes, glowing blood red. It was looking straight at us, but it flew toward the town.'

'We went straight home. My friend was shaking as he bolted the door shut; he couldn't believe what we saw. Finally, he convinced himself it had just been an optical illusion; until he saw the News and the Nuclear disaster was reported.'

There are other reports of a Mothman creature being seen at an area of swine flu outbreak. Engineer Fransisco Torres told *Inexplictica* investigators that people had been seeing a tall creature, over nine feet tall, with huge wings and red eyes in La Junta, Mexico.One witness, a young student at the North Region University, who asked them for confidentiality, claims that the strange entity even chased him. He said that he was driving home after class one evening when he saw something in the road ahead of him. It looked like a man, hunched over and wrapped in something. Then suddenly it stood, and taking two steps it opened a huge pair of wings and flew toward the young man's car. It kept apace with the car as the student tried to drive faster to escape it until after several minutes of sheer panic, the enormous 'bird like' thing flew away.

In September 1978, workers arriving for their shift at a coal mine in Freiburg, Germany, saw a tall man standing in the opening of the mine, wearing a trench coat. As several of the coalmen approached him to see he wanted, they were suddenly stunned to see a cape-like cloak unfurling around the man. Then they began to feel the most terrible horror as they realized it was no man standing there. As the 'cloak' unwrapped they realized it was a pair of huge wings, uncovering the body that was not human. The scream it then emitted chilled their blood and hurt their ears.

Reports were that it "sounded like fifty people screaming all at once;" others said it was more like a train screeching on tracks as though the brakes had been applied in emergency. Recoiling in utter fear and horror as it stood motionless in front of them, the miners retreated from it. They remained some distance away from it for a long time, until it disappeared inside the mine entrance. Very reluctant to enter inside, the miners continued to stay out of the mine, until suddenly they were all thrown to the ground by a huge explosion coming from inside the shaft.

When the mine inspectors arrived to investigate the damage the explosion had caused inside, they were adamant that had the miners been inside at the time of the explosion, they would all have been killed.

Speculation rose that the creature, though terrifying in its appearance had come to warn them and to prevent them from going to their death. Others felt the creature had somehow purposely caused the explosion.

Esoteric Philosopher of the 1920's Geoffrey Hodson, claims to have experienced a terrifying visitation that he believed was a 'nature spirit.' Going on to write a book about Fairies, he was to describe this experience in detail in it. He was hiking alone in the picturesque Lake District of Cumbria, when suddenly in front of him appeared, "a huge crimson bat-type thing about twelve feet high with burning eyes. It was not human but like a bat with outstretched wings, and a human face. As soon as it felt itself observed, it shifted into its shape, with its piercing eyes upon me." Then it disappeared, only to return again, this time in a smaller form, he claims.

In March 2005, numerous residents of Santa Fe in Argentina called the police with perturbing reports of seeing a baffling character who became called, "The crazy roof man." All independent witnesses said the same thing; that he was some sort of cat-man, who performed the most athletic of maneuvers in front of them, leaping from roof-top to roof-top with astounding super-human agility. Each report put him at over seven feet tall, clothed in black, and with some kind of cape and stick. Some said it was as though he was a comic book hero come to life, with legs so long he could jump across streets with a single bound and scale walls with ease.

One woman claimed that after the silhouetted figure pointed at her, his eyes red and his gaze intense, she lost all ability to move. Perhaps the shock paralysed her, though she hinted at something more powerful than that. Others claimed the figure would simply de-materialize in front of their eyes. Dora Ruiz claimed to have seen it prancing on the rooftops. No features of his face could be determined other than glowing red eyes. One resident exclaimed that he had fired numerous shots at the figure with his gun, only to see it completely unaffected by the direct hits. In fact, it howled back at the man and continued to jump around on the roof tops, as though taunting him. The police were alerted but they could not catch it. He leaves no trace, other than scratches along the walls from his long fingernails. Though sightings eventually ceased, whatever it was it was never apprehended....

Barry Chamish, a leading UFO researcher in Israel, reported on the bizarre case in 1997 of a young girl, Suha Anam, who had to be rescued by neighbours in the Dir AL Awasan district when an 'alien' creature tried to snatch her from her second-floor balcony. The case was reported to the police and apparently the incident was recorded in their reports.

She was standing alone on the balcony at the back of her apartment when 'an alien' suddenly appeared out of no-where and began tugging her by the arm, trying to pull her with him. Screaming in hysteria, her neighbours heard the commotion and came quickly to her aid.

Telling the police about it, one neighbour said she heard the screams and the sounds of what she thought were like a helicopter. When she looked out of her window to see what was happening, she says she saw whirling in the air and an ash-like substance filling the air. The girl was treated in hospital for scratches and shock.

Then, that same week, two other people say they witnessed 'aliens.' Schoolboy Muhand, 16, said that he was walking his usual route home when he saw an odd-looking man in the road; but it wasn't a man, he said, "the skin was the colour of a frog. It had only three fingers on its hands." With its hands the boy said it came toward him trying to scratch at his face. In terror the boy watched as it then screamed something indecipherable at him and suddenly flew into the air.

Before this incident, another man came forward to say that he had seen something in the sky that had 'the figure of a man with arms and legs.' Police took all of the accounts seriously and even went so far as to set up some kind of ambushes to try to trap the entities before they could cause serious harm; but they did not catch it....

Chapter Fifteen: A New Sentient Intelligence

As insane and crazy as it sounds, a highly unusual, sinister and sentient entity seems to have been discovered in the last thirty years, according to some conspiracy researchers. Something that appears to have its own intelligence. Put simply, it's a black substance, called by those who have studied it 'black goo,' for want of a better term.

It's an oil-like substance that some conspiracy theorists believe was the real reason England went into the Falklands War in 1982. David Griffin of Exopolitics UK claims that there was a hidden reason for War. It was not a war over territory but instead was driven by the need to seize this powerful biomorphic substance.

It's thought to be some type of sentient being. It exists not just as a physical fluid, but also as an intelligent morphogenic energy that has consciousness. It is multi-dimensional.

This living intelligent organism hibernates in temperatures below freezing, but if it is exposed to warmer temperatures, it becomes active. It can then attach to anything; including animals and people.

Some researchers say that this 'goo' comes from an Alien base in the area. It was allegedly seized by the British during the War with Argentina and exported to English laboratories to be studied in the hope of weaponizing it. It is not definitively known whether that was achieved or not.

Its purpose is said to be for use in 'the end times,' and conspiracy theorists such as Broadcaster Miles Johnston of 'The Bases' you tube channel has been interviewing people who say that 'factions' of the Government/Military are creating hybrid beings by injecting them with the black substance, altering their DNA.

U S Veterans Today senior editor Gordon Duff, a global intelligence specialist has written about this black substance too, with a different explanation from his sources. 'The Nano-substance had been activated by a device from an off-planet location. It has become sentient and aggressive. It has shown itself capable of disarming fleets and killing people.

He says the Military, *so far*, have been able to protect us, through their use of 'technologies', but the Chinese are in league with a "group" that are able control this substance. Intelligence agencies believe that the Chinese are acting to try to 'control' us for an off-world civilization that they have a 'relationship' with.'

He says that China has spread a rumour that it has an ethnic bio-weapon capable of killing all 'non-Mongolian' people, and has asked other Countries to ally with it.

As though to silence doubters, he then points out that 'America has had diplomatic relations with an 'off world' civilization for at least fifty years, and anyone who lives in denial of these factors are as crazy as the 9/11 deniers.'

Witnesses Miles Johnston has interviewed say it was discarded by the British military as unpredictable. The rumours are rife. If any of it is true, then more than one Military Industrial complex may have it. It's alive, it has its own intelligence, and it may soon develop its own agenda....

It will either be used for nefarious means against parts of the world population, or it will break free on its own, and if it does, no-one knows what devastation to human life it will cause.....

Insane conspiracy theory....or something more......?

Excerpt from **_Taken in The Woods by Steph Young_**

Here follows the correspondence from Suzie, received a few weeks ago; 'I saw what you are going to be discussing on the show on Coast to Coast tonight and I felt you might be interested in reading about what I witnessed a few years ago. I wrote to Dave Schrader to ask him to pass this info to you. I am writing you to ask you to take a look at my own personal report. It scares me to this day and I feel it's important to get the word out about this. I do not know if those entities are still there to this day, but I hope people can be alerted to the fact that these things are out there.

My sister moved to a different town since then and I have not been back to New Hampshire. I wish someone would go check it out because these things are totally invisible and who knows where they are, or where they went.

Anything that was that intelligent and in tree tops needs to be investigated in my opinion. I try not to think about it too much because it could freak me out. I hope this report helps people stay safe. Something is out there for real and we can't see it with our eyes at all!'

This is Suzie's account; she was staying at her Sister's home in a wooded subdivision of Hampstead. It was spring 2003 and it had been rainy the last few days. Often late at night, Suzie would go out onto the front deck to smoke. She described that each night, as she sat on the deck after midnight, she would hear large sticks breaking in the forest. It happened every night.

Being a seasoned camper and having been brought up by Scout leaders, she didn't think anything of it at first, but she did notice that she never heard any rustling of leaves, but she brushed it off as being some kind of animal.

But night after night the sounds continued, and she could also hear the sounds of scraping on the tree bark and of something dropping out of the trees. She would look into the forest for any kind of movement but couldn't see anything there. The porch and driveway were well lit by the flood lights. She used a flashlight to beam light into the trees. But she couldn't see anything at all moving.

Then the sounds started to move closer. The longer she stayed out on the porch the closer the sounds started to come.

In the daylight, she checked the trees for any marks and looked for animal tracks. She sent her nephew out into the woods to jump on sticks to measure the sound she was hearing at night. He could only break smaller sticks but Suzie could break the large ones by jumping on them. This implied that whatever was doing it was larger than an 11-year-old boy; yet Suzie didn't know of any animals that large whose habitat was in this area.

Not only that, but at night they were coming closer to the house. Getting her nephew to move around in the woods, she was able to estimate that the distance the sounds were coming from had to be no more than 20 or so feet away from her.

And, she knew there were more than just one of 'them,' because at night the sounds would come from the front of the house and from behind at the same time. They were coming from two directions simultaneously.

Yet they were not visible to human sight, and they weren't showing up on any photographs she'd taken, but even inside the house now Suzie began to feel like she was being watched.

On the laptop at night, sitting by the curtainless window, she felt like she was being observed. The dogs were picking up on something too, because from their basement crates they would start howling.

Then one night Suzie was outside on the porch again when she heard them coming. Again, the floodlights were lit up and she could see the panorama of trees clearly, but she could see nothing there and there was no rustling; only sticks breaking, and they were coming closer.

About eight feet away from her, some plants stood in pots on the lower part of the deck, and she watched as the plants moved to one side and then sprung back into place, as though something had brushed past them, except nothing was there that she could see and there were no other sounds like footsteps, or the sound of steeping on grit.

The night had no wind or breeze, but the flowers had been pushed aside a significant distance. Whatever it was, it had come up the stairs toward her. In absolute shock, her head running through what she'd just seen happen, she turned and ran inside, locking the door hurriedly.

Shortly after that incident, she was sitting by the window on the computer again when the eerie feeling of being watched returned. As she looked at the living room wall she thought she could see shadows above it on the ceiling, as though someone had just walked past, but everyone was in bed. She thought it had to be her imagination playing tricks and she decided to take a shower and relax. The bathroom was situated across from the basement, which was closed. When she finished her shower and came out of the bathroom, the basement door was open. As she went upstairs she saw her nephew's bedroom light on but he was fast asleep in bed. She believes it's possible that whatever it was outside had somehow got into the house.

How did they get in? She's not sure; "Through the walls, the basement door?" But she wants to know what they are, and why they are interested in humans? She says, "I'm a person who's been through a lot and has seen and experienced a lot in life; I don't scare as easily as others which is why I stood there so long and why I went back night after night to listen and see if I could see them. There was no movement whatsoever visually, and it was reasonably well lit. No-one in my sister's house was up late and outside so they had never experienced this before and they tried to make all kinds of excuses for it, like it was the trees popping from the cold weather or small animals. I wish I had had equipment to record it."

"I was only about 4-5 feet from the door the whole time. I wish I'd been able to get my brother-in-law to stand out there with me. He's a total non-believer in anything unexplained. Too science based. All things are explainable to him. Oh and a tiny aside, I tried to flip my cigarette in their direction but it didn't fly right and I lost that opportunity and fled. I wanted to see if it would bounce off of whatever was there."

"Were they just watching? testing? hunting? Or abducting? On the grass there's no sticks; they're silent. How many other homes did they go into? There were no other sounds and no communication of any kind. Not even telepathically. These things are either inter-dimensional entities, or cloaked, or perhaps out of our visual range of ability to see. We need to learn about them as fast as we can so we're not caught with our pants down. I had no other way to get my story out back when it happened. Calling into shows is hit or miss and paranormal forums only reach a small portion of society. I know they are still out there, I just know it."

"It would be different entirely if I were not well versed in camping, forest sounds. I easily can rule out a lot because of my background. All animals of the forest rustle dry brush and leaves on the forest floor even a little bit when they are trying to be quiet. I am a seasoned camper who was raised by scout leaders camping a lot in my life. I know the forest sounds and the animal behavior."

"A lot of people initially accused me of making up a scary story; they didn't believe it was real. Then they made every forest animal the source of the sounds as if I don't know about regular animal sounds. Of course, a few said it was Bigfoot because they believe he can go invisible. I know beyond any shadow of a doubt this was no Bigfoot. Bigfoot breaks trees and beats on things. He walks heavy and rustles the foliage and dry leaves on the forest floor. This was quiet creeping and no rustling at all. I know a coyote howl from a wolf, and the sounds that fox and raccoon make."

"Through further discussion on a paranormal website a few things came to light. One person suggested the sound wasn't actual breaking sticks but a sound they make. Who's to say? One person interpreted the situation that the entities were testing me to see what I'd do. This comment/thought made my hair stand up straight and I have long hair! This put a twist on it that had not occurred to me before. Prior to that I thought the entity accidentally brushed the flower as it passed closely by it. If it were done intentionally to observe me, that involves high intelligence and that really means we are up against something ...frikin' scary as hell."

"This will haunt me the rest of my life. I hate that. I feel that way out of pure fear. Terror in fact. I know in my gut this is going on everywhere and has not been discovered yet. I can add this too, they were up in the trees for a reason.

To me, they hunt at night. They go in the trees to watch like hunters in a tree stand. This means hunting/observing in my opinion. Question is, are they documenting or planning dinner?"

"I really haven't been the same since. I never feel okay in the woods anymore even in the day light, though I have not had many chances to get out in the woods in recent years. Hell, I don't feel safe in my own yard especially at night. We all need to track these things because they pose a threat in my opinion. This was nothing normal at all. These things were sneaking up on me, synchronisticaly. They had obviously communicated to each other in some way to be so perfectly in sync. That's what really scared me bad. It showed high level of intelligence. Question is, were they sneaking up to observe me, or to stalk me? Was I prey or to be captured, or just observed? THAT is what made me run inside and lock the door."

~~~

Excerpt from *Something in the Woods is Taking People* by Steph Young

'Something in the Woods is taking people. Something unknown that we cannot define; something that others have had the misfortune to encounter. People snatched soundlessly, never to be seen again. Or returned; dead. A strange and highly unusual predator. Highly intelligent. Very successful. And able to overpower someone in an instant.

This is a puzzle. An often deadly one. Here follows some very troubling and disturbing accounts....

Fatal accidents can happen very easily to even the most experienced climbers, and in the wilderness, hikers can get lost in an instant. A couple of wrong turns and they can be lost immediately. A slip on a rock or a trip near a crevice and death or serious accidents can come quickly.

Falling into a creek or down between a pile of rocks, a body; dead or injured, can be hidden from search parties quite easily. However, with highly trained tracker dogs and heat seeking infra-red equipment to detect a person's body heat, the mystery often remains as to why people are not found, or are found in the most unusual of circumstances.

Natural predators can lurk in the wilderness; bears, cougars, and occasionally a hiker will be victim to these wild animals. They feed where they kill, or drag their bloody victim to a nearby lair; they leave a trail that is obvious to searchers.

However, the victims in this book show no evidence of an animal attack.

For these victims, there is no logical explanation.... only enigma and many questions...

Something in the Woods is taking people....

People taken; sometimes returned, but never the same again.

~~~

The Disappeared

In July 2012, sixty-six-year-old Michael LeMaitre was the subject of a huge search effort in Alaska that was to last several days. He'd completed many marathons and was competing in the Seward's Mount race. Last spotted by race organizers approaching the mid-point of the race, on a busy main trail, they expected him back at the five kilometers finish shortly after. He was never seen again.

Despite thorough and intensive searching with tracker dogs, they could find no trace of him and no scent to follow. Thermal imaging equipment searched for signals of his body, yet none could be found. Hundreds of volunteers took to the area, searching every possible crevice for over ten days.

How could he disappear in so small a spot they all wondered, running a planned round route of just 5k and surrounded by other runners? They were mystified by finding absolutely no trace of him.

He disappeared without trace. Every crevice was searched. He left no scent to track. It's almost as though he was plucked into the air. He certainly wasn't on the ground anymore...

* * *

In July 2006, student Aju Iroaga was standing alone on a country road just by Lake Superior, having stormed off-site of a tree planting project.

He'd been told to re-do the trees he'd just planted and he was angry. He'd already re-done his work once, and he was exhausted. Now he was stuck there, in the middle of the forest, several kilometres from the company base. He'd been told if he was quitting, he'd have to wait for the team to finish and then he would be taken back to the base to get his belongings and leave.

He waited for nearly four hours, just standing there, and was last noticed still there at about quarter to four in the afternoon. At 6pm when the team finished however, he had disappeared. Concerned, the supervisors and team looked around for him, two of them even staying there that night in case he turned up.

Police officers arrived at about 11 pm, and at dawn they began their search with helicopters and K9 units to pick up the student's trail. However, the dogs could find no scent of him. The police's original theory was that he'd decided to walk through the wilderness to the camp. They had nothing else to go on; but no footprints or scent to track either. He was never seen again.

At one stage, the Ontario Police suggested that because he was a fit young man, he may have run an access road the length of over *60km* to the Trans-Canada Highway to hitch a ride. Despite how fit he was it seems a highly unlikely theory.

A website put together by the heartbroken family says, "That there is no evidence of foul play, and no evidence that he walked off, leaves an unacceptable mystery. People simply do not vanish."

The co-owner of the company he was there working for was quoted as saying, "He was certainly strong enough, both in will and physically to be able to take care of himself." Where did he go? And what did he meet that was stronger than him?

* * *

In June 2013, the Reiger family from Oklahoma were on vacation in Ecuador. The family decided to take a short hike from their hotel, along a scenic trail. At some point along the hike, the two boys ran on ahead but only one of them returned.

The elder son it seemed had disappeared into thin air. The boys were close to each other on the hike, separated only momentarily when the elder had vanished.

"The really strange thing about it is," his father told newspapers, "that whatever happened to him was in the space of five minutes; we were right behind him. You couldn't get lost. The whole of the trail is visible. If he was hurt, he would have been seen."

Searchers could not seem to locate the boy's tracks, and indeed stated that they didn't detect any other tracks in the boy's vicinity either. No-one heard him shout or scream, no sounds of any thrashing in the undergrowth or of a fall, no blood, no scent.

Army troops were called in and the Soldiers rappelled down the ravines, tracker dogs, fire-fighters, and volunteers from the village below joined in.

Some have suggested, given that they could not find a body in the ravines, and that they couldn't detect his scent, that the most logical thing that could have happened was that he was suddenly 'lifted' from the ground by something. It's as though he was somehow 'disappeared' into invisibility.

"I could see; I was there. I don't know why they didn't find him. He would have been seen. I cannot come up with a scenario that makes any sense. Nothing makes any sense," says his Father.

* * *

'A hiker's disappearance adds to hundreds of others,' wrote an Oregon newspaper in 2013.

They'd discovered that an astonishing figure of two hundred and forty people were recorded as missing after going into the Oregon wilderness since the late nineties. Highlighting just two of the cases, they related how a former member of the United States Coast Guards had disappeared in the Willamette National Forest in 2012.

His profession had depended on him being extremely fit and athletic, and he kept up his level of fitness after leaving with frequent hikes and cycling. However, once he entered the national park he was never seen again. Nor were any of his belongings, including an inflatable raft and his cell-phone. Bodies will sadly succumb to the elements, but other things are more durable; they don't decompose. They weren't found either though. Jake's mother told the reporter, "There's a mystery here. Both were experienced. Two grown men can't simply disappear."

She was referring to six years prior to this, when a professor of mathematics at Oregon University, Dr. Xu, went hiking near the spot where her son Jake had been. No sign of him has been seen either. The search had covered one hundred miles of the forest using tracker dogs and heat seeking equipment. For a while they followed footprints that were thought to be his, but the trail suddenly stopped.

How can a trail suddenly stop and yet there be no explanation as to where he had gone from there?

Searching for Explanations:

Travel writer Logan Hawkes talks of having encountered shadowy entities in the Big Bend National Park. He describes how, a few years ago as he was travelling through it with a friend, they stopped at the hot springs to relax in the water for a while and enjoy the peaceful beauty of the area as it grew to darkness around them.

Finally it became pitch dark and they stared up at the sky counting the stars. Suddenly they could see what looked like silhouetted shadows of a group of people, standing on a ledge away up the river. He and his friend expected the group might approach them and became a little anxious. They waited with trepidation, knowing no-one else was around for miles.

Finally, after not seeing them move and hearing no sounds of talking coming from them, they shone the flashlight over at them to see them more clearly. "Except there were no figures in the light; then turning the light off the faint silhouette outlines re-appeared."

Unnerved after repeating the exercise a couple more times and seeing the same response, they didn't hang around and quickly climbed out of the water, keen to get their clothes back on and get out of there. "To this day we cannot say who or what they were. But I can confidently tell you they were not living beings."

Texas isn't the only State where these elusive and hard to define 'shadow beings' have been seen. In the Santa Lucia Mountains along the central coast of California, it was known that the Native Americans told of 'Dark Watchers'; shadowed figures who would appear on ledges as dusk fell into night. Human-like ghost figures, always dark shadows, standing silhouetted against the landscape.

Who they are, and what they want no-one knows, but many have seen them. Usually it seems they disappear without coming any closer. Many have speculated about them, and others have told of their encounter in forums on the internet.

'Weird California,' has a collection of compelling and highly mysterious contributions from witnesses who have written in to tell of their sightings; L Brennan of Ramona, wrote: "While flying my aircraft I glanced toward the Range and saw what looked to be seven very large dark figures standing there."

"We saw a very large dark figure," says another, "standing at the edge of the mountain, staring off into the distance; it was over 10 ft. tall. It seemed to have a cape, with broad shoulders... extremely weird; I travel that road daily. This was around September 2010." In a slightly different account, G Garner says, "We see them here; they're almost like horses on their hind legs in the dusk."

In Missouri too there's been sightings in a place that's called 'Zombie Road,' near the Mahoning River not too far from Ohio. A photo exists of what appears to show a group of Shadow People, standing along a tree line above a small lake. It was taken in March 2005 by paranormal investigator Tom Halstead prior to his death. There are no reflections of their bodies in the water below. It seems from accounts of those who have reportedly seen them, that 'The Watchers' are less sinister than the 'Shadow people.' While the Watchers do not seem to interfere with humans, unless those who have encountered them up close are no longer around to speak for what happened, it would seem that they prefer to be left alone.

Shadow people however, according to medium Toiny Braden, "Are evil and full of malicious intent; those are the ones you never want to see. I've felt such intense levels of malice," she says, of the ones she's seen around her when assisting clients, they've been terrorizing.

Excerpt from *Terror in The Night*

The Gurning Man

A rarely told Scottish tale, 'The Gurning Man,' evokes terror just by its very name.

Accounts started to circulate about this figure in the City of Glasgow. In particular, it seemed to be centered on the district of Crosshill. For three years, females reported sightings of this entity at night. They said it looked, 'demented,' and 'insane.' When it made an appearance, it was allegedly of human shape, and solid-looking.

Many of the women who did encounter it were reportedly so afraid and traumatized that they actually moved away from the area, to ensure that they would never encounter it again. *British Paranormal* site relates one account from a woman in her fifties who lived with her husband and children. She was woken one night by a strange snorting sound. Opening her eyes, she saw something at the end of the bed. It looked like a man, but from the light through the curtains, she watched as he grinned at her in the most maniacal fashion while bizarrely rubbing his hands fast up and down his chest.

Letting out a blood-curdling scream, her husband woke up and on instinct he rushed from the bed to turn the light on. Confused and perplexed, he turned to his wife and asked her what on earth was wrong; the strange man in the room had disappeared. There was no-one there.

Perhaps her experience could be put down to a nightmare; however, without her knowing, only a few days prior to this, two girls in their teens had reported their own horrific encounter and it was very similar. Their incident happened within close walking distance of this lady's house.

The two girls had been walking home late one night after a party. There was a near-full moon and so, though it was dark they could see quite well as they walked. Suddenly they saw a man in front of them, whose appearance was decidedly strange. In their estimation, he looked to be perhaps in his fifties, bald, and almost skeletal due to his extremely thin frame. He was all in black. What they also found disconcerting was that his movements were jittery, as though he were incredibly agitated.

As they drew nearer, they began to feel the hairs on the back of their necks stand up and they fell into terrified silence as they looked at him. Walking as quickly as possible past him, they turned again to look at him and were stunned by the oddest expression on his face, which they described as being a contorted combination between a grimace and an unnaturally wide grin. Not only this, but he was making the most awful snorting sounds and grunting at them.

They took off running as fast as they could, looking back over their shoulders in fear that he would chase them, only to find that he had completely disappeared into thin air. There was no possible way, they said, that he could have gone so quickly out of sight, in mere seconds. There was no-where for him to have hid and the road behind them was wide and empty.

Then there were more reports; an elderly woman saw him standing in the middle of a road, looking agitated and jittery. In front of her eyes, he was gone. Police were called to one home where the occupiers believed it was a burglar, yet the figure disappeared in front of them. There were over fifteen separate sightings from witnesses, who had no prior knowledge of the other reported encounters. Then the reports stopped. The riddle of the entity was never solved. Perhaps it was figments of all of their imaginations, or perhaps it simply moved to another location... Could this perhaps be the same kind of entity as described by many who have seen 'the *grinning* man?'

In a peculiar account told in Ronald Pearson's '*Table Rappers*,' by a Mrs. Sidgwick, a keen psychical researcher in the 1870's, two sisters and a maid were returning from evening service in a village church. Moonlight lit their way though fog hung in the air. Suddenly they heard a man whistling behind them; then they heard his footsteps. As he neared them, it seemed that he passed directly *through* one of the women. Suddenly, there were more people around them; a mass of people. Some seemed to rise out of the ground. They were short and dwarf-like. "We saw two men that appeared to grin, looking hideous and so close to us, and my companion said in horror, 'I can't walk past that,' and I answered: "Look at the sky and you won't see them."

One man was twice as tall as any of the others. He kept pace with the women, walking with them with long, noiseless strides, towering over them until they arrived home, shaking and completely terrified...

~~~

Excerpt from *Haunted Asylums, Morgues & Cemeteries.*

Eric and his friends, John and Claire, first went to the imposing derelict psychiatric hospital one night in the early hours for a bit of 'fun.' They had felt compelled to go and visit the old Barrow Gurney hospital. "We were laughing and joking with each other; it was just for fun. We just walked round and we didn't see anything."

Then they reached a courtyard inside the building and suddenly the atmosphere changed dramatically. "By this time it was 3.30am, but my watch had stopped. It was quite creepy. We had a camera with us and took a few pictures quite randomly. Then we started to hear a muffled sound of voices. We didn't want to go back inside the buildings and so we left, but I felt Claire being physically pushed forward. When we got home we looked at the photos and they seemed to show balls of light at some of the windows. When we looked closer we could see they were human faces."

Unable to get what had happened off their minds, a few weeks later they were unable to resist the temptation of going back. They took the camera again and a torch. Again back in the dark grounds of the derelict hospital they took nearly two hundred pictures. "We didn't even look at the picture viewer at the time; we just took them, but when we got home we couldn't believe what we could see," says the 52-year-old property developer to the local Bristol News.

The images appeared to show a man in a window holding a cross, as well as other faces in the windows, and a large hooded figure in a dark corridor. There are orbs in nearly all the photographs and the building itself seems to appear shrouded in mist even though the night was clear and crisp. "The air felt atmospheric; almost like what you feel in the Tropics." Despite seeing the large and menacing shrouded figure in the hallway, and the face in the window, or perhaps because of this, they were becoming addicted to going there and they returned for a third time.

This time, things seemed to become even more sinister. "There was a massive shadow over the building; we could see shadows running in and out of the hospital. I saw a figure standing by one of the doors. It was jet black yet with a white head, but it had no face. It was 'watching' us. I have struggled to accept the things I saw there those nights but whatever is there, it's not human."

They sent the pictures to the Psychical Research Society, yet so far they are unable to explain exactly what the pictures have captured. "We aren't 'trick' photographers," he says, as though to ally the inevitable claims from sceptics, "and we are not in any paranormal groups."

There is the feeling that a lot more happened at the hospital than has been fully described so far, because Eric adds: "This is just an overview of the incidents. There was a prolific amount of activity. Let it be said that whatever me and my friends stumbled upon is beyond anything we know. I don't know how or why, but I do believe that something has arrived there recently. At least part of this 'arrival' is intelligent; it's able to interact as blatantly as it wants. I hope it has gone back to where it came from. This isn't a joke."

He ends cryptically and ominously, "The truth is, few could even begin to understand what the pictures prove the existence of."

~~~

I hope you have enjoyed this book and the strange collection of mysterious events. If you have enjoyed it, perhaps you would be kind enough to leave me a review,

Thank you so much,

Steph

These intriguing cases are just the beginning....... there are many others in the collection of books I've written....Added to this, I have a Podcast, called "Masquerade Podcast with Steph Young." If you would like to, you can listen to Episodes on iTunes, or here for; **New & Exclusive Episodes:** https://www.patreon.com/stephyoungpodcast

I have website; http://www.stephyoungauthor.com/ if you would like to subscribe to my mailing list, to stay up to date with new releases.

Who is Steph Young? Steph is a frequent guest on radio shows & podcasts including appearances on the National Radio show 'Coast to Coast AM,' as well as many more...

Steph Young is an independent researcher, addicted to researching all Supernatural, Paranormal, Esoteric and enigmatic Mysteries. Each book she writes seems to lead her to further questions and searches for answers, as the unexplained Mysteries inevitably deepen & develop into ever more complex riddles in the spectrum of the Unknown.

Steph Young now hosts a Podcast on iTunes. "Masquerade podcast with steph young" discussing creepy mysteries of the Unexplained," covering all unexplained mysteries, unexplained disappearances, all things paranormal, encounters with the unknown, unsolved mysteries, and of course, creepy things that happen in the woods...

Free Episodes are now up on iTunes, or more episodes are on Patreon steph young podcast

If you have experienced something strange and unusual like this, that's hard to explain, please feel free to let me know. I'm actively continuing to research and would be very interested to hear from you, at my website or stephenyoungauthor@hotmail.com

I hope you have enjoyed this book and the strange collection of mysterious events. If you have enjoyed it, perhaps you would be kind enough to leave me a review,

Thank you so much,

Steph

Also by Steph Young:

https://www.amazon.com/Steph-Young/e/B00KE8B6B0

The Strange Case of the Smiley Face Killers

Something in the Woods is Taking People

Unexplained Disappearances & Mysterious Deaths: True Tales

Monstrous Monsters & Creatures: True Stories of Gothic Macabre

HORROR in the WOODS -Unexplained Disappearances

Experiences of Afterlife Communication-Evidence of the Afterlife

Mysteries of the Macabre: True Stories featuring the Corpse Brides and more

And many more ....on Amazon

GOTHIC MACABRE:
MONSTROUS TRUE
TALES

Printed in Great Britain
by Amazon